THE CROCHET ANSWER BOOK

The
Crochet
Answer Book

2nd Edition

Solutions to Every Problem You'll Ever Face

Answers to Every Question You'll Ever Ask

EDIE ECKMAN

Storey Publishing

The mission of Storey Publishing is to serve our customers by publishing practical information that encourages personal independence in harmony with the environment.

Edited by Gwen Steege and Sarah Guare
Art direction by Mary Winkelman Velgos
Text production by Erin Murphy
Indexed by Nancy D. Wood

Cover photography by Mars Vilaubi
Illustrations by Brigita Fuhrmann
Fabric care symbols created by the American Cleaning Institute,
    www.cleaninginstitute.org

Storey Publishing
210 MASS MoCA Way
North Adams, MA 01247
www.storey.com

Printed in China by R.R. Donnelley
10 9 8 7 6 5 4 3 2 1

LIBRARY OF CONGRESS CATALOGING-IN-PUBLICATION DATA

Eckman, Edie.
  The crochet answer book : solutions to every problem you'll ever face : answers to every question you'll ever ask / by Edie Eckman. — 2nd edition.
    pages cm
  Includes index.
  ISBN 978-1-61212-406-3 (flexibind with cloth spine : alk. paper)
  ISBN 978-1-61212-407-0 (ebook) 1. Crocheting—Miscellanea. I. Title.
TT820.E35 2015
746.43'4—dc23
                                                                2014033696

Once again, and always, to Bill, Meg, and Charles, for their unwavering support and love, and to Tyler, for keeping me company

Contents

(Appendix, continued)

All You Have to Do Is Ask!

It's been almost ten years since I first attempted to answer the questions most often asked by crocheters, and in that time, as they say, a lot has changed. Electronic devices are always at hand, crochet's popularity has grown, Ravelry was born, and crochet patterns are often presented in graphic (symbol) form.

At the same time, not that much has changed. Crocheters still have questions; they harbor insecurities about where to put the hook, how to maintain the required number of stitches, how to determine gauge, and how to read a pattern. Some are afraid to crochet a garment or step outside their comfort zone. Furthermore, many, many crocheters don't even know that there *is* more to know about crochet — more refined techniques that they could use to make their work look better.

Crocheters are often free thinkers, blazing their own way and discovering new and inventive techniques without benefit of outsiders. This is wonderful, but how much better would it be if we could somehow channel and capture that knowledge in order to share it with others? Sometimes these new discoveries are wheel reinventions: old techniques that haven't been well disseminated, perhaps from lack of distribution channels (no longer a problem in the age of the Internet), and perhaps from a lack of a standard vocabulary. One of the challenges for crocheters, now and in the past, is the lack of a standard terminology for crochet techniques. We can't even agree on a label for basic stitches, so how can we effectively share our knowledge with others, or even be confident in what we think we know?

Today, most people head straight for the Internet when they want to know something, but there is value in having a reference of curated information. Books like this one allow you to get your question answered and at the same time be drawn to other related (or non-related) techniques. You can flip through the pages and land on helpful information at any turn.

In my opinion, being a "good" crocheter is not about making perfectly stitched, elaborate, artful creations. It is rather a matter of confidence. You need to be sure of what you are doing and how to do it, and then have the confidence to figure out what to do if things aren't going quite right. Understanding why you do certain things and why they turn out the way they do increases confidence and leads to successful crocheting. The more you learn, the better you become, in crochet as in life.

When you have a question, use this book as a primary source, or simply visit it from time to time when you have a spare moment. I've tried to answer some of the most common questions crocheters have and to anticipate some questions you didn't know you had. Chances are, you'll find your answer here, and possibly be directed to helpful sites to learn more. Even if you're a complete novice and want to learn to crochet, you can do that using this book (see Quick-Start Guide, page 12.

Since I wrote the first edition, I've written an entire book on crocheted edgings, and two books on crocheted motifs. Through research for my books, as well as teaching, I've learned a lot, and I've adapted and added content to this new edition accordingly. You'll find more information on symbol crochet, Tunisian crochet, and, of course, edgings and motifs. However, there's still a chance I've omitted your most burning question or left out your favorite technique. I'd love to hear about your unanswered questions or how you have solved your own problems. Many of the new questions and answers in this edition come directly from reader and student questions. You can find me online at www.edieeckman.com, as well as on the usual social media channels.

It is my hope that *The Crochet Answer Book* will lead you down the road to gaining the confidence that makes for good crocheting.

Quick-Start Guide for New Crocheters

Although this book is not organized in sequential steps as a "learn to crochet" book, it is certainly possible to learn the basics (and more!) from the questions and answers presented. If you are just getting started, grab some smooth, light-colored worsted weight (#4) yarn and a 5 mm (H/8) hook, then use the following questions as a tutorial:

▶ How do I make a slip knot? (page 70)

▶ How do I hold the hook? (page 17)

▶ How do I hold the yarn? (page 20)

▶ How do I make the foundation chain? (page 71)

▶ Does it really matter which way I wrap the yarn over the hook? (page 71)

▶ What should I do if I'm having trouble getting the loop on my hook over the head of the hook? (page 72)

▶ How do I keep the growing foundation chain under control? (page 73)

▶ Where in the stitch do I insert my hook into a foundation chain? (page 77)

▶ How do I make a single crochet stitch? (page 91)

▶ How do I make a double crochet stitch? (page 96)

▶ What does fasten off mean? (page 114)

You'll have other questions, of course, but by the time you've mastered the topics above, you should be well on your way to exploring on your own.

CHAPTER 1

Get a Grip . . . on Hooks and Other Tools

One nice thing about crochet is that you need only two things: a hook and yarn. Of course, there are many other useful tools and accessories that can make your crocheting life more enjoyable. Let's explore some of the many options, beginning with the hook.

All about Hooks

Q What are the parts of a hook?

A There are several different hook styles, but each has four parts: a tip or head, a throat, a shank or shaft, and a thumb rest.

throat   *shank or shaft*

tip or head —

thumb rest

Q What are the differences among hooks?

A Hooks are made of plastic, metal, wood, nylon, or bone. Some have a thumb rest; others have a straight shank with no thumb rest. The handle may be cushioned or shaped. Some have an inline head, while others have a tapered head with a tapered throat. When you crochet with thread, you use a steel hook that may be so tiny that you can barely see the shape of the head.

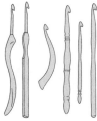

hook variations

And those are just the regular hooks! There are also specialty hooks. Hooks used for Tunisian crochet have a long straight shank that resembles a knitting needle. Double-ended hooks have a hook at each end of a long straight shank. Interchangeable hook sets allow you to connect a range of different size hooks to a long cable for even more flexibility when working Tunisian or double-ended crochet.

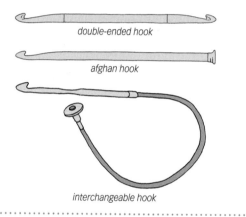

double-ended hook

afghan hook

interchangeable hook

Q With all the choices available, how do I know which hook is best?

A Choose the style hook that is most comfortable for your hand. It should be of good quality, with no rough spots. Some people prefer to work with a certain brand of hook or with hooks made from a certain material. The length and shape of the hook handle should also be comfortable for the way you hold and manipulate it. And, of course, the size of the hook should be appropriate for the yarn or thread you are using. No matter what type of hook you have, the shank is the major determining factor in the size of the stitch.

You may find that you prefer different types of hooks for different yarn and stitch patterns. Slippery yarns like rayon might be easier to manage with a "sticky" wooden hook, while fuzzy yarns might work up faster when you use a slick aluminum hook. You may have a preference for an inline head rather than a non-inline head.

. . . .

Q **What's the difference between an inline head and another kind of head?**

A An inline head (often called "Bates" style) is one where the head of the crochet hook is no wider than the area in which the stitch is formed, while a non-inline head (often called "Boye" style) is larger than the shank to one degree or another. While no particular style is best, most crocheters have a strong preference for one type of head over another; it's a matter of personal preference.

inline head

non-inline head

Q How do I hold the hook?

A Hold the hook in your dominant hand in the way that is most comfortable for you. The most common ways to hold a hook are shown below. If you hold the hook a different way from those shown, and it works for you, then don't feel you must change your technique.

LEFT-HANDED   RIGHT-HANDED

pencil hold

LEFT-HANDED   RIGHT-HANDED

knife hold

Q **How are hooks sized?**

A Hook sizes are described differently in different countries. Often U.S. terms include both letters and numbers; the UK and Japan each have their own numbering systems. Metric labeling is the most consistent and accurate way of describing hooks, since it is a measurement rather than a numbering system.

In the United States, standard crochet hooks range from U.S. size B/1 (2.25 mm) through jumbo size S (19 mm). But beware! Hook sizes may vary from manufacturer to manufacturer. There is no guarantee that one company's size H/8 (5 mm) hook is the same size as another company's, even when both are described in metric terms. In addition, numbering systems have changed over time, even with hooks from the same manufacturer. It is always best to use a hook gauge to determine the size of your hook in metric terms.

The steel hooks used for thread crochet have their own numbering system, from a tiny Japanese size 16 (.4 mm) upward.

Q **What size hook do I need?**

A Published patterns and yarn labels suggest a hook size, but this is only a starting point. You should always stitch a swatch to check your gauge. If you need to change

Hook Sizes

This chart is a compilation of hook and size ranges from various sources. Keep in mind that the great variation of numbering systems over the years and from brand to brand can greatly confuse things. For example, a comparison of hook charts from a number of sources lists a 4.0 mm hook as either a G/6 or an F/5. If you aren't following a published pattern, match the hook to the yarn or thread you are using: Larger yarns require larger hooks. Most yarn labels suggest an appropriate-sized hook for that yarn.

STEEL HOOKS

MM	U.S.	JAPAN
0.4		16
0.45		
0.5		14
0.55		
0.6		12
0.7		
0.75	14	10
0.85	13	
0.9		8
0.95		
1	12	6
1.1	11	
1.25		4
1.3	10	
1.4	9	
1.5	8	2
1.65	7	
1.75		0
1.8	6	
1.9	5	
2	4	
2.1	3	
2.25	2	
2.75	1	
3.25	0	
3.5	00	

STANDARD HOOKS

MM	U.S.	JAPAN	UK
2		2/0	14
2.25	B/1	3/0	13
2.5		4/0	12
2.75	C/2		
3		5/0	11
3.125			
3.25	D/3		10
3.5	E/4	6/0	9
3.75	F/5		
4	G/6	7/0	8
4.5	7	7.5/0	7
5	H/8	8/0	6
5.5	I/9		5
6	J/10	10/0	4
6.5	K/10.5		3
7		7	2
8	L/11	8	0
9	M/N 13	9	00
10	N/P 15	15	000
15	P/Q		
16	Q		
19	S		
20		20	

from the suggested hook size in order to get correct gauge, then by all means do so. Having the correct gauge is always more important than using the suggested hook size.

SEE ALSO: *Pages 155–69 for working a swatch, pages 42–43 for Yarn Weights with Recommended Hook Sizes and Gauges.*

Q **How do I hold the yarn?**

A The yarn from the ball needs to be tensioned through the fingers of the hand not holding the hook. The end of the yarn attached to the hook goes over your forefinger. The yarn should move freely through your fingers while still being within your control. You may want to wrap it under and over other fingers in addition to your forefinger, or wrap it twice around your forefinger or pinkie. Experiment with ways to tension the yarn so that it is comfortable for you. Don't worry if it feels awkward at first; with practice it will feel more natural.

Some people choose to hold both the yarn and the hook in their dominant hand, and throw the yarn over the hook as if they are knitting. This is not ideal; try to learn another method unless you are efficient and confident with your current method.

LEFT-HANDED   RIGHT-HANDED

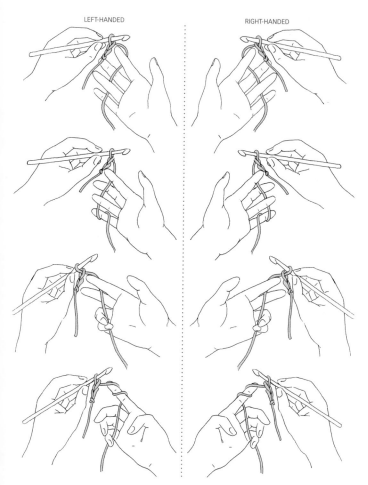

four ways to hold yarn

Q My mother and my friend hold the hook and yarn differently. How do I know which is correct?

A Neither is the only correct technique. It's okay to hold the hook and the yarn in any way that is comfortable to you, even if it's not one of the ways illustrated here. As long as you are happy with the consistency of the stitches and are comfortable while you are crocheting, you are correct.

Q When I crochet for more than an hour, my hands and shoulders start to ache. Is there anything I can do to prevent this?

A Sitting still and being hunched over our crochet (or our computers) for hours at a time is not a good idea. It's really best to crochet in smaller chunks of time, with plenty of break time in between. There are a number of precautions you can take to prevent injuries from cutting into your crocheting time.

▶ Use a hook that's comfortable for you. You may enjoy using a hook with a cushioned handle or a specially shaped grip. Hold the hook and yarn gently, and try varying the way you hold them. If you normally use the pencil hold, try the knife hold at least some of the time.

▶ Keep your shoulders relaxed, down away from your ears, and support your shoulders and back. Don't hunch forward or slouch! Allow your work to rest on your lap so that you aren't holding its weight with your hands. You may find it helpful to place pillows under your arms while you stitch.

▶ Take frequent breaks to rest and stretch. Set a timer to remind yourself to get up and stretch every 30–45 minutes or so. Stretch your fingers out as far as possible for a count of 10, and then make a clenched fist for a count of 10. Repeat this several times. Rotate your wrists clockwise, then counterclockwise. Shrug your shoulders up and down and in circles. Clasp your hands together behind your back and squeeze your shoulder blades together to open your chest.

▶ Listen to your body. If you are holding tension anywhere, or if something starts to be uncomfortable, stop! It really is more important to take a break than to finish that granny square right now.

▶ Fingerless gloves or therapeutic gloves may help by keeping your hands and wrists warm.

▶ Most important, if you experience tingling or numbness in your hands, or if you have persistent discomfort, stop and consult a health-care professional. Crocheting should never hurt.

. . . .

Q Can I crochet left-handed?

A Certainly. Hold the hook in your left hand and the yarn in your right hand, and stitch from left to right, instead of right to left. If you are learning from a right-handed crocheter, or following a published pattern, you may have to make some adjustments, as most instructions are written for a predominantly right-handed world. If a right-hander is teaching you to crochet, sit opposite and mimic the actions you observe; you'll be crocheting left-handed. Some books contain illustrations for both right- and left-handed stitchers; in this book, we have tried to offer both wherever appropriate.

You can follow illustrations for right-handed crochet by holding a mirror to the side of the illustration, or by scanning the illustration into your computer and flipping it horizontally on a graphics program. Because you are working from left to right, the shaping of some pieces will take place on the "other" side of the garment. In other words, if you follow cardigan instructions for the Right Front, you'll be making the Left Front.

NOTE: *To avoid copyright infringement, make copies for your own use only.*

Some left-handed crocheters find that they can work just fine holding the hook in their right hand as right-handers do. If you can, just stitch "right-handed," and avoid the hassle of translating your patterns to left-handed crochet.

Filling Your Tool Bag

Q **What other tools do I need?**

A Although a crochet hook is really the only tool you must have, a number of others are useful. You may want to keep a little tool bag handy, filled with some or all of these other practical tools:

▶ **Small, sharp scissors.** These come in many styles. Keeping them at hand saves time and frustration.

▶ **Tapestry needles.** Also called yarn needles, these blunt-tipped sewing needles have large eyes. They come in several sizes; you'll want at least two sizes to correspond to the size of the yarns and threads you use most often.

▶ **Measuring tools.** You'll be less tempted to cheat on measurements if you keep a tape measure and a ruler at hand. A tape measure is good for measuring bodies and large projects; a ruler is best for measuring swatches and flat fabrics.

▶ **Hook gauge.** Use a hook gauge to determine the size of unmarked hooks. The hook gauge contains a series of holes in graduated sizes. The holes are numbered in both metric and U.S. terms. Slide the shank of your hook into the smallest hole it fits, then read the corresponding number to determine the size of the hook.

▶ **Stitch markers.** Available in a variety of styles, markers work better than pieces of yarn to mark stitches, as yarn can leave unwanted bits of fuzz in your fabric. Avoid the round markers meant only for knitting; you need a type that can be opened so you can hang it on a stitch and easily remove it later.

▶ **Coiless safety pins and/or locking stitch markers.** Similar to safety pins, coiless safety pins don't have the yarn-grabbing circle at the far end. These and other types of locking stitch markers are useful for marking stitches, holding pieces together for seaming, or keeping track of increases and decreases.

split ring
stitch marker

coiless pin

additional marker styles

▶ **"Personal discomfort fixers."** Hand lotion, lip balm, and a nail file can prevent annoying interruptions to your stitching sessions.

▶ **A calculator.** This is an important tool if you are doing your own designing, or adapting another's design. It can also come in handy for checking the math in a pattern if you run into a problem.

▶ **Note-taking tools.** Keep a pen or pencil and paper handy to remind yourself where you are and what you have done. Get into the habit of making notes to yourself as you work. You may need to repeat something (or avoid it) later.

▶ **A row counter.** This comes in handy when row counts are important and you are working a stitch pattern that is difficult to keep track of, or when you are using a fuzzy yarn that just defies counting. You may also want to use it when working sleeve shaping, or to ensure you have the same number of rows on the left and right fronts of a cardigan. There are row-counting apps available for your electronic devices.

▶ **A variety of crochet hooks in different sizes.** If you have alternatives near at hand, you are more likely to keep swatching until you get the right gauge.

SEE ALSO: *Pages 155–69 for swatching.*

▶ **A latch hook.** Use this great little tool for weaving in ends too short or too bulky to fit into a yarn needle.

latch hook

▶ **Smartphone or other electronic helper.** A smartphone can act as your calculator, as well as a note-taking

tool and row counter. There are all kinds of helpful apps
and features that make your phone a useful crochet tool.

. . . .

Q I'm really into crochet. Are there any other tools
that make the work easier and even more fun?

A There's always something more! Ask for these great
tools for your next birthday.

▶ **Magnifying glasses/reading glasses.** If you are a certain age, and haven't yet discovered the joy of reading
glasses for close work and small print, give these a try.
Yarn and craft stores also carry magnifying glasses on
a stand, or ones that hang around your neck and rest
against your chest.

▶ **Blocking wires and a blocking board.** Tools used in
the final finishing stages of crochet, blocking wires are
sturdy thin wires than can be threaded through the
edges of a crocheted fabric to keep the edges straight.
A blocking board is a type of surface that is used in the
blocking process.

SEE ALSO: *Pages 298–306 for blocking.*

▶ **A ball winder and yarn swift.** These tools, used together or separately, are wonderful time savers for winding hanks of yarn into flat, center-pull balls. You can also use the ball winder to rewind your

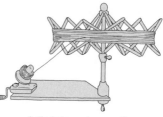

ball winder and yarn swift

yarn if you have to rip out a large expanse of stitching.

▶ **Daylight lamp.** This is a special light bulb that emits full spectrum light. These bulbs can help you choose colors and make it easier to see dark stitches in the evening. Some companies make a combination lamp and magnifying glass.

▶ **Hook cases.** Use these to corral and organize your hooks. Unfortunately, it's still up to you to put them away when you are finished!

▶ **Pompom maker.** Pompom makers are an inexpensive luxury. You can certainly make pompoms using cardboard circles, but if you are going to make a lot of them, pompom makers are a treat.

CHAPTER 2

A Good Yarn

Luckily for us, there is a seemingly endless variety of yarns on today's market. However, with this diversity comes the matter of choice. Which yarn is best for which types of projects? Understanding the characteristics of various yarns will help you determine the answer.

Kinds of Yarn

Q What is yarn made of?

A Animal, plant, and synthetic fibers are all used to make yarn. Animal fibers include silk produced by silkworms, wool from sheep, alpaca from alpacas, qiviut from the musk ox, angora from rabbits, and mohair from angora goats (go figure!). Plant fibers include cotton from cotton bolls, linen from the flax plant, and ramie from an Asian shrub. There are also yarns made from soy, bamboo, pine, corn, and other plants. Acrylic, nylon, polyester, and other synthetic fibers are man-made, in some cases from recycled materials. Lyocell (Tencel) and rayon are man-made fibers produced from cellulose, which is a natural material. "Metallic" yarns are usually a synthetic, metallic-looking fiber spun with another fiber.

. . . .

Q What are some of the common terms used to describe fiber characteristics?

A All of the following terms will help you understand and describe the fibers you work with:

▶ **Absorbency.** The ability of the fiber to take in water
▶ **Breathability.** The ability of the fiber to allow air to pass through it

▶ **Dyeability.** The ability of the fiber to accept and hold dye

▶ **Hand/handle.** The way a fiber feels, a tactile description that may include words like soft, fine, harsh, stiff, resilient. The hand of a fiber influences the hand of the fabric that it is made into; the fabric might additionally be described by its "drape."

SEE ALSO: *What is drape?, page 207.*

▶ **Loft.** The amount of air between the fibers; lofty yarn is usually lighter in weight than its thickness implies. "Fuzzy" yarn is lofty.

▶ **Resiliency (elasticity).** The ability of a fiber to return to its original shape after being stretched or pulled

▶ **Thickness.** The diameter of the fiber, measured in tiny units called microns

Q Why does fiber content matter?

A A yarn's characteristics, such as its resiliency, hand, loft, absorbency, and dyeability, are largely determined by the fibers that make up that yarn. Being familiar with the features of different fibers helps you make appropriate selections when you choose yarn for a project. You might decide, for instance, that while a luxurious alpaca throw is an excellent choice for your mother, a washable acrylic-blend yarn is a more suitable choice for your four-year-old son's afghan. Knowing the fiber content of a yarn is also important when it comes time to launder your finished project.

. . . .

Q **What are fiber blends?**

A Often fibers are blended to take advantage of the best properties of each one. For example, acrylic might be blended with wool to make the yarn machine washable while maintaining the breathability of the wool fiber. A 50 percent alpaca/50 percent wool blend maintains the luxurious feel of the alpaca but is more affordable and more resilient than a 100 percent alpaca yarn.

The fiber with the higher percentage of content in the yarn dominates the yarn's characteristics. An 80 percent cotton/ 20 percent wool blend looks like a cotton yarn, but it is lighter weight than a similar, all-cotton yarn would be.

. . . .

Q **How is yarn made?**

A The initial processing depends on the fiber. Wool, mohair, and alpaca are shorn from the animals, resulting in a fleece made up of staples (short strands similar to locks of hair). Angora rabbits are combed or clipped to remove their hair. Cotton bolls that look somewhat like the cotton balls in your bathroom cabinet are harvested from cotton plants and processed through a gin to remove the seeds. Silk comes off the cocoon of a silkworm in a continuous filament; these filaments may be cut into manageable lengths before they are processed. To make rayon, cellulose from wood or cotton is processed into a solution called viscose and then extruded through tiny nozzles to form the rayon fiber. Tencel is a cellulose product made from tree pulp, processed in an environmentally friendly manner. Other man-made fibers are produced in a single, long filament but are often cut into staple-like lengths before spinning to more closely resemble the properties of natural fibers.

Before the fibers are spun into yarn, they are combed or carded in order to align the fibers. At this point, they may be blended with other fibers. The fibers are then spun together into an S twist or a Z twist, depending on which way they are turned. The twisted strand, or ply, is spun with one or more other plies in the opposite direction to make a multi-plied

2-ply yarn   *3-ply yarn*

S-twist and Z-twist

yarn. Plying fibers adds strength and balance to the yarn. Sometimes the plying step is omitted, however, resulting in a yarn made of one twisted strand, known as singles. Most commercial yarns are spun by machine, but you may also be able to find some lovely handspun yarns. Dyeing may take place before the yarn is processed (referred to as dyed in the fleece), as carded/combed fibers, or as finished yarn.

. . . .

Q **What are the characteristics of wool that make it so very popular?**

A Wool is warm, insulating, resilient, breathable, water-repellent, dirt-resistant, naturally flame-retardant, and it takes dye well. Different breeds of sheep yield wool with different characteristics. It is weaker wet than dry, but it can absorb up to 30 percent of its weight in moisture without feeling wet. It may felt if subjected to heat, moisture, and friction. Some manufacturers make wool machine-washable by treating it to the "superwash" process.

SEE ALSO: *Page 217 for information on felting.*

Q **What are the best-known characteristics of cotton?**

A Cotton is inelastic, heavy, absorbent, and non-insulating and takes dye well. It has a tendency to stretch, although it may also shrink when washed. It is usually machine-washable and is stronger wet than dry.

- -

Q What's special about alpaca?

A Alpaca fiber is soft, strong, breathable, and water-repellent. It is more insulating than wool fiber, so it is warmer than wool of the same weight. It comes in many natural colors, as well as dyed colors.

- -

Q What makes mohair so appealing?

A Mohair is durable, resilient, strong, and soil-resistant. It accepts dye well and is very warm for its weight. The staples are long and lustrous.

- -

Q What makes synthetics so useful?

A The range of synthetic fibers is so vast that it is necessary to generalize. Manufacturers continually attempt to make synthetic yarns that mimic the best properties of the natural fibers. Synthetics are usually durable, water-resistant, strong, non-breathable, non-wicking, and non-insulating.

Many synthetics are machine-washable. Most are very sensitive to heat and melt or burn at fairly low temperatures.

. . . .

Q **What is the difference between yarn and thread?**

A Crocheters use both terms, sometimes interchangeably. Thread is generally thinner, and usually made from cotton, silk, or linen. It is often used for bedspreads, doilies, and lace. Yarn is everything else! In this book, I use the word "yarn" for both, unless otherwise stated.

Yarn Facts and Figures

Q **What do I need to know about yarn size?**

A For years, publishers and yarn manufacturers have attempted to come up with meaningful classifications for the size of yarns, and knitters and crocheters have attempted to pigeonhole yarns into these classifications. Most recently, *weight* has been the determining factor, but we must be careful with the term because it is used in this case to mean thickness, or the yarn's diameter. (Yarn diameter is also called *grist*.) In reality, how much a yarn actually weighs is less meaningful than its diameter and loft. The diameter of the yarn is one of the most important words we can use in effectively describing yarns, yet we still call it weight. Some yarns, such as brushed mohair, have a relatively small diameter compared to their loft (the amount of air between the fibers, or the amount of space the yarn occupies). In other words, the fuzzy bits of the mohair make it a heavier "weight" yarn than it would be without fuzziness.

The table on pages 42–43 gives the generally accepted yarn types in the United States. In the United Kingdom, New Zealand, Australia, and other countries, the same names may refer to different-size yarns, or you may run into different terms altogether.

. . . .

Q I've heard yarn described by its "wpi." What's that?

A Spinners and weavers use the abbreviation "wpi" for "wraps per inch," which is a way of determining yarn size (weight). The more wraps per inch a yarn has, the smaller diameter it is. The wraps-per-inch measurement helps take into account the loft of a yarn as well as its diameter, although it is a somewhat subjective measurement and various resources disagree on which wpi measurements fit into which weight categories. Wraps per inch should *always* be used in conjunction with other information in determining yarn characteristics.

Q How do I measure wraps per inch?

A Make two marks exactly 1 inch apart on a pencil, dowel, or specially made wpi tool. Wrap the yarn evenly around the pencil or dowel between the marks or inside the notches of the wpi tool, taking care to wrap the strands parallel and adjacent to one another, not too tightly, not too loosely. The number of wraps you can count in that 1-inch space is the wpi. For more accuracy, wrap over 2 inches and divide the resulting count by two. You can also use a ruler, although it is harder to wrap evenly around a ruler.

Q How is thread size described?

A Thread is generally described in numbers ranging from a superfine, truly threadlike size 100 to a more yarnlike size 3. The higher the number, the smaller the diameter of the thread. Thread may also be categorized by the number of plies. Some threads are more tightly spun than others. Many cotton yarns are mercerized or subjected to a chemical treatment that adds strength and luster.

Q How is yarn packaged?

A Yarn is sold in put-ups of skeins, balls, or loose hanks (also called skeins). A hank (or skein) of yarn is loosely wound, usually from a reel or swift, then tied in several places. You must wind it into a ball before working with it. Balls and commercially wound skeins are neat packages that you can use immediately. The weight of the put-up varies but is commonly 1.75 oz (50 g) or 3.5 oz (100 g). You may find synthetic yarns put up in larger quantities.

Q What information can I find on the yarn band?

A Whether packaged in skeins, balls, or hanks, most yarn or thread is labeled with information on the fiber content; suggested gauge; weight and/or yardage of the skein, ball, or hank; laundering instructions; dye lot; color number; and possibly a color name. Many American yarn bands include the Craft Yarn Council yarn weight designation. Suggested crochet hook and knitting needle sizes and gauge are also often included.

SEE ALSO: *Page 318 for information on laundering instructions;*
pages 42–43 for more yarn weight information.

Q What do all those icons on the yarn band mean?

A These are international symbols that provide the information described in the previous answer, even if you can't read the language on the band. The icons are especially helpful if you purchased an imported yarn. Information on the suggested gauge and hook/needle sizes may also be shown in graphic form.

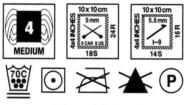

typical yarn label information

SEE ALSO: *Page 388 for more on yarn care symbols.*

Q What is a dye lot?

A Yarns are dyed together in large batches or dye lots of the same color. Each dye lot is numbered, so you can tell if two skeins of yarn were dyed at the same time in the same batch. There can be subtle or not-so-subtle differences between dye lots.

Yarn Weights
with Recommended Hook Sizes and Gauges

STANDARD YARN WEIGHT SYSTEM	TYPES OF YARN	RECOMMENDED HOOK SIZE IN METRIC (US) TERMS
0 LACE	Fingering, 10 count crochet thread, laceweight	Steel hooks 1.75 mm and smaller
1 SUPER FINE	Sock, fingering, baby	2.25–3.5 mm (B/1 to E/4)
2 FINE	Sport, baby	3.5–4.5 mm (E/4 to 7)
3 LIGHT	DK, light worsted	4.5–5.5 mm (7 to I/9)
4 MEDIUM	Worsted, afghan, Aran	5.5–6.5 mm (I/9 to K/10.5)
5 BULKY	Chunky, craft, rug	6.5–10.5 mm (K/10.5 to M/13)
6 SUPER BULKY	Bulky, roving	9 mm (M/13 and larger)

ADAPTED FROM: *The Craft Yarn Council's Standards & Guidelines for Crochet and Knitting and Ravelry's Standard Yarn Weights.*

RECOMMENDED GAUGE IN SINGLE CROCHET, OVER 4" (10 CM)	UK/NA/AU EQUIVALENTS
	1–3 ply
21–32 sts	3–4 ply
16–20 sts	5–8 ply
12–17 sts	8 ply
11–14 sts	10–12 ply
8–11 sts	12–16 ply
5–9 sts	16–20 ply

Q Does dye lot really matter?

A Many times it matters a great deal. Even if the dye lot differences are not apparent in the packaged ball or skein, they often show up in the finished project. Whether it matters in your project depends on how close together you use same-color yarns of different dye lots. If they are adjacent, you probably shouldn't mix them, as even subtle dye lot differences show. However, if the yarns are separated by another color, it is probably safe to mix dye lots in the same item.

When purchasing yarn for a project, your best bet is to be sure that all of the same-color yarn comes from the same dye lot.

Q How do I know if the yarn colors I've chosen will look good together?

A In the store, hold them together and squint. Try to do this in daylight, not under fluorescent lighting. At home, wrap each of the colors around a white index card side by side, in the same proportions that you will use them in the finished project. Look at the card critically. Are the colors pleasing together or is one of them jarring? Can you put them next to each other in any order? Is there one that shouldn't be adjacent to another? If you are satisfied with the results on the index card, try all the colors together in a swatch.

You may also want to learn more about color theory. Entire books have been written on the subject, and it can be a life-long study. The short answer is, if *you* like the colors together, that's what really matters.

SEE ALSO: *Pages 155–69 for swatching.*

Q I found the perfect color, but my yarn store doesn't have enough skeins from the same dye lot to complete my project. Do I ever dare use different dye lots in the same project?

A Try some of these ideas for minimizing problems when using different dye lots:

▶ Separate the different dye lots with a stripe of a different color.

▶ Switch stitch patterns where the dye lots change. Often a difference in texture can hide a slight color change.

▶ Use a stitch pattern that mingles the stitches and rows by working in rows below or over other stitches and thus avoids straight lines of stitches of different dye lots.

▶ Make the odd dye lot a separate element, such as a pocket, collar, or border.

▶ Work a chain stitch or other surface embellishment over the spot where the dye lots meet.

Q Why are some yarns labeled "No Dye Lot"?

A These are synthetic (man-made) yarns. The chemical process allows producers to get exactly the same color results every time they produce a fiber in a particular color.

Yarn Substitutions

Q Can I use a different yarn than the pattern calls for?

A Yes, but you'll need to use a yarn similar to the one the pattern calls for to get similar results. Because of their unique properties, novelty yarns may be tricky to substitute in a pattern, but ordinary yarns can often be substituted quite successfully.

SEE ALSO: *Page 60 for novelty yarns.*

Q How do I find a substitute yarn?

A Try these suggestions for evaluating a substitute.
  Compare data about the yarns. Start by noting what you know about the original yarn. What weight is it? What gauge does the pattern call for? What is the suggested hook size? Then, look at the yarn you'd like to substitute and make sure it is the same weight as the original yarn.

(Remember, this refers not to how much the packaged yarn weighs but rather the weight classification.) The yarn band gives you the suggested gauge and hook size for the new yarn; you should be able to crochet the new yarn to the same gauge as stated in your pattern.

Consider other characteristics of the original yarn. What is the fiber content? Is it a plain yarn? Fuzzy? Smooth? Bumpy? Stiff? Tightly or loosely spun? A loosely spun yarn or a single-ply yarn will look different from a yarn with a tighter twist or multiple plies, even if they are the same weight. You should be able to determine these characteristics from the description in the pattern or from some online research.

Consider the characteristics of the item you are going to make. Is there lots of textured patterning that would not show up well with a variegated or slubby yarn? Is it a lacy item that works best with a natural fiber that can be properly blocked?

Buy a single ball of the new yarn, if possible, and swatch with it to ensure you are happy with the results. You may not mind if the substitute yarn is not exactly the same as the original, but it's best to make informed choices. If you are unsure, check with a knowledgeable sales clerk where you buy your yarn.

Q My pattern calls for 3-ply wool. Will any 3-ply wool be sufficient?

A Not necessarily. In the past, yarns were often categorized according to the number of plies. This worked because there were a limited number of commercially available yarns, and everyone understood a 3-ply yarn to be of a certain diameter. These days, it is not sufficient to describe yarns by ply alone, as some multi-ply yarns are very fine and some singles are ultra bulky. You'll need to determine the weight classification of the original yarn and choose an appropriate substitute.

SEE ALSO: *Pages 42–43 for yarn weight classifications.*

Q Can I buy yarn by weight?

A If you're referring to its weight classification, then the answer is, "Probably." If you mean you want to figure the amount of yarn you need to buy based on how much each skein weighs, then the answer is, "Bad idea." Buying by skein weight is another holdover from the past, when most yarns were wool and of a fairly uniform size. Length (yardage) is what matters, not how much the yarn weighs. Cotton yarn weighs more per yard than wool; some wools weigh more per yard than others. If yardage is not listed on the ball band, see if you can determine it from the Internet or other sources so that you buy sufficient yardage for your project.

Q Can I use two lighter weight yarns together to make a heavier yarn?

A Yes, but you'll have to work a gauge swatch to see if you can get the correct gauge. To get off on the right foot, try using this rule of thumb: Add the suggested gauge of each of the two yarns and divide by 3 for the suggested gauge of the two yarns held together.

For example: Using two strands of sport-weight yarn with a suggested gauge of 4 sc = 1", double the gauge of the yarn and divide by 3:

$$(4 \times 2) \div 3 = 2.67 \text{ sc} = 1"$$

If the gauge you are expecting to use is in the ballpark of 2.5 sc = 1", then you might be able to use those two strands of sport-weight yarn together. Don't forget that you'll need a larger hook than you would for a single strand of sport-weight yarn. You'll probably start with the hook size listed in the pattern instructions. Swatch with your proposed yarn and hook to see how close you are. If you are using a yarn doubled, remember that you'll also have to double the amount of yardage called for in the pattern!

SEE ALSO: *Pages 155–69 for swatching.*

Q If I'm substituting yarn, how much do I buy?

A Figure out how much yardage you need by multiplying the number of skeins the pattern calls for by the number of yards or meters per skein of the original yarn. You should be able to find this information in the pattern instructions. Once you know the total length you need for your project, divide that number by the number of yards or meters per skein in the yarn you want to use. You'll probably get a fraction. Be sure to round up since you cannot buy a fraction of a ball of yarn.

For example: My pattern calls for 8 skeins of Pretty Yarn (100% acrylic, 200 yds/100 g). I want to use Beautiful Yarn (100% wool, 240 yds/4 oz) instead. Here's the math:

8 skeins × 200 yards = 1600 yards

1600 yards ÷ 240 yards = 6.67, or 7 balls

You may want to buy one additional ball for safety's sake. Remember, you'll be using up yarn making a good-size swatch.

Be sure you are using consistent units of measure (yards or meters). If one yarn is labeled in meters and one in yards, you'll need to convert the meters to yards or vice versa before calculating how much yarn you need. It's not as important as it is in rocket science, but differing units can trip you up.

Q **Do you have any advice on how much yarn I'll need when I'm designing my own projects?**

A That's the six-million-dollar question, isn't it? The amount of yarn you need depends on the size of the yarn, the stitch pattern, your gauge, and the size of the item you are making. Of course, when you follow a published pattern, the instructions are your guide. Many people regularly buy an extra ball of yarn, just to be certain to have enough. You can always use leftover yarn for another project, and many stores accept returns of extra balls for credit. If you don't have a pattern to go by, find a published pattern for an item similar to your design, using a yarn of similar weight, and estimate your needs. You can also estimate your yarn needs when you make your swatch.

Q **How do I calculate yarn amounts from a swatch?**

A You'll need to calculate the yarn weight or yardage used in the swatch, then apply that to the finished measurements of your intended project.

Measuring by swatch weight. This is possibly the most accurate method. (For advice if you don't have access to a scale, see the next question.) Make a swatch at least 6" square, using the same colors and hook you plan to use in the project, and with the intended gauge. Do not trim or weave in your yarn tails. Calculate the area of the swatch by measuring width times length. Don't round off your measurements, and be sure to include partial inches! Weigh the swatch on a food scale or postage scale and make a note of the number of grams it weighs. (Grams is a more accurate measurement than ounces.)

For example: My swatch weighs 20 g and measures 6 × 6.5 inches = 39 square inches. My yarn comes in 100-gram skeins of 220 yards each.

Now, estimate the total area of your project in square inches. It's easy if your project is a square or rectangle: just multiply the width times the height. If you're making a sweater, the calculation is a bit more complicated; see page 255 for that formula.

For example: For an afghan that measures 48" wide and 60" long,

$$48" \times 60" = 2880 \text{ square inches}$$

Use these formulas to calculate the number of balls needed:

$$(\text{Weight of swatch} \times \text{Total area of project})$$
$$\div \text{ Area of swatch} = \text{Total weight for project}$$

$$\text{Total weight for project} \div \text{Weight of 1 ball}$$
$$= \text{Number of balls needed for project (round up!)}$$

For example: Using the numbers from the examples above,

(20 g × 2880 square inches) ÷ 39 square inches = 1476.9 g

1476.9 g ÷ 100 g = 14.77, rounded to 15 balls

Since this is an estimate, you might want to buy 16 balls just to be safe. And of course, if you are using multiple colors, you may need more than this, depending on how the colors are distributed. Estimate what percentage of each color is used in your swatch, and multiply that percentage by the total amounts, then round way up to allow for estimating errors. Remember, you can't buy a partial ball of yarn.

If you want an estimate of actual yardage, multiply the calculated number of balls times the number of yards per ball.

14.77 × 220 = 3249.4 yds

If you don't have access to a scale. Before you begin the swatch, pull out a length of yarn (say, 5 or 10 yards or meters), jot down the measurement, and tie a loose overhand knot. If you reach the knot before completing your swatch, untie the knot, reel out more yarn, jot down the new measurement, and tie another loose knot. When the swatch is complete, measure how much yarn is left before you get to the knot. Subtract this amount from the total of the length that you pulled out of the ball. This is the length you used for the swatch, including yarn tails. And yes, you could just rip out the swatch and measure the yarn used, but then you won't have the swatch to refer to.

SEE ALSO: *Pages 155–69 for swatching.*

For example, a 6" × 6½" swatch used 44 yards. How much yarn is needed for a 48" × 60" afghan using yarn that has 220 yards per skein?

Get the total yardage needed for the project using the following formula:

(Yardage in swatch × Total area of project)
÷ Area of swatch = Total yardage for project

(44 yds × 2880 square inches)
÷ 39 square inches = 3250 yds (rounded up)

3250 yds ÷ 220 yds per ball = 14.77
Rounded to 15 balls (or to 16, if you want to be safe)

. . . .

Q How do I convert from yards to meters?

A One meter equals 1.09 yards, so divide the number of yards by 1.09 to get the conversion to meters.

For example: To convert 15 yards to meters:

15 ÷ 1.09 = 13.76 meters

Or just ask the nearest electronic device.

Q How do I convert from meters to yards?

A Reverse the process and multiply the number of meters by 1.09. Another way to think of it is that it takes about 10 percent more yards than meters.

For example: To convert 25 meters to yards:

$$25 \times 1.09 = 27.25 \text{ yards}$$

SEE ALSO: *Page 396 in the appendix for metric conversions.*

Q My pattern calls for a yarn that has been discontinued. Is there any way to find out about the characteristics of discontinued yarns to help me choose an appropriate substitute?

A There are resources available to help you find out more about yarns, even those that are discontinued. With luck, the pattern will list information such as weight, yardage, and fiber content to help you make substitutions. Local yarn shop owners often have information on discontinued yarns, and very experienced ones may even be able to play "Name That Yarn" with just a glance. You can also search the Internet. Sellers on eBay often offer older yarn, complete with fiber and yardage information. Try Google or other search engines for the yarn name and manufacturer. Try contacting the yarn manufacturer. As of the time of this writing, www.ravelry.com

and other sites have information and reviews on yarns, both current and discontinued.

Working with Yarns

Q **What is the best way to pull yarn from the ball?**

A Usually pulling from the center is best. If you are using a commercially packaged skein or ball, first look to see if the outside strand of the yarn is tucked into the center of the ball. If it is, pull it out but don't use it. Stick your fingers into the center of the ball and fish around to see if you can find the inner end. You may need to pull out a little wad of yarn and unravel it in order to find the tail. This is the end to use as it will draw from the inside of the skein.

commercially wound ball

NOTE: *If you are working with the yarn doubled, you may use both the end from the center and the one from the outside of the ball.*

Q How do I handle a loose hank or skein of yarn?

A Don't try to work directly from the hank or you'll be sorry! You need to wind it into a ball before you start stitching. You can use a yarn swift, lampshade, chair, or someone willing to hold the yarn for you. Untwist the hank and hang it carefully on your holder. If the yarn is tied in several places, cut the shorter pieces of yarn and throw them away. Sometimes there is a single knot where the beginning and end meet, wrapped in such a way as to keep the yarn from tangling. Be especially watchful in the beginning, because you may have to unwrap the yarn from around the skein for the first few revolutions. Cut the knot, and take a single end in your hand, winding carefully for the first round or two until you are certain that the yarn is unwinding without tangling.

SEE ALSO: *Page 29 for more on ball winders and swifts.*

Q Can I create my own center-pull ball?

A Yes. The easiest way is with a ball winder, which winds the skein into a nice center-pull form. If you don't have a ball winder, however, you can do it manually:

1. Hold the starting end between your thumb and forefinger and spread your other fingers. Keeping the tail secure with your thumb, wind the yarn in a figure eight around your

fingers about a dozen times. Don't let the strands overlap each other.

2. Pinching the yarn where it crosses itself, slide the yarn off your fingers.

3. Fold the bundle of yarn in half.

4. Keeping 10–12 inches of the tail end dangling, start winding the yarn loosely around this little wad of yarn, turning it this way and that to form a ball. Wrap the yarn over your fingers as well as over the ball of yarn to ensure that you are wrapping loosely enough. When you have finished winding, you should be able to pull on the tail coming out of the middle of the ball.

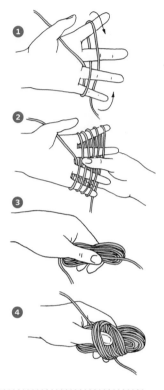

. . . .

Q How do I know if my ball is wound too tightly?

A Your ball should not be hard — it should have a bit of spring to it. Yarn wound too tightly is stretched and tense, which is apt to cause trouble once it's made into a fabric. The yarn may become permanently stretched, decreasing its elasticity. Even if it isn't permanently ruined, if you stitch the yarn up in its stretched state and then wash it, it will return to its natural, unstretched state, with possible undesirable consequences to the size of the piece! If you wind a center-pull ball, the ball collapses in on itself as it is used, releasing any extra tension.

....

Q How can I keep my yarn from splitting?

A If your yarn splits, it may be that the yarn is not of high quality or that it is loosely spun. Some hooks with pointy tips may split the yarn. In that case, you may need to stitch extra carefully to avoid splitting the yarn, or use a different hook. A hook with a rough spot also sometimes causes trouble. Try sanding the rough spot with very fine sandpaper. If that doesn't work, discard the hook.

If your yarn is coming untwisted as you work, examine how you are pulling it from the ball. If you are using a center-pull ball, you may be removing twist because of the direction you are pulling. Try pulling from the opposite side of the ball or using the end from the outside of the ball.

Q What should I do when I reach a knot in the yarn?

A Even high-quality yarns may have a knot or a weak spot every now and then. Don't work over it. Instead, cut the yarn several inches before the knot, leaving a tail to be woven in later. Cut out the bad spot, then begin again, just as you would when adding a new ball.

When you begin a new row, pull out enough yarn to work the entire row, so that you can see any imperfection before you reach it. You can then cut the yarn and rejoin it at the beginning of the row and thus avoid starting a new yarn in the middle of the fabric.

SEE ALSO: *Page 65 for starting a new yarn.*

Working with Challenging Yarns

Q What is a novelty yarn?

A Just as its name implies, this isn't your run-of-the-mill yarn. You'll know it when you see it. The fun of a novelty yarn comes from its unique characteristics; it can be made from almost anything and spun in almost any way. It may have a great deal of texture, or it may be spun with non-fiber additives such as beads or feathers. It may have little bits of stuff hanging from a main core. It may be a thin "crochet along" (or "knit along") thread meant to be held together with another strand of yarn as you stitch, or it may be as bulky as your thumb.

Novelty yarns are often described by their characteristics: eyelash, slub, metallic, ribbon, or bouclé (meaning *curly* in French). When substituting one novelty yarn for another, choose a similar yarn type in order to achieve a similar look.

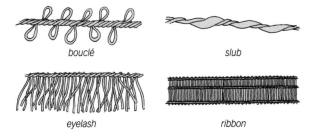

bouclé

slub

eyelash

ribbon

Q I've tried working with novelty yarns but found them frustrating. Do you have any suggestions?

A Novelty yarns and fuzzy yarns are beautiful, but they can present a challenge for crocheters. Here are some tips that may make it easier if you are using a novelty yarn:

▶ Use your fingers as well as your eyes to determine where to put the hook.

▶ Work between stitches rather than into actual stitches. (If you are following written instructions, be aware that the gauge and look of the fabric will be different from fabric stitched in the standard way.)

SEE ALSO: *Page 119 for working between stitches.*

▶ Work with a larger hook than you normally would use for the weight of your yarn. Again, pay attention to your gauge if you are following a printed pattern.

▶ Try a mesh stitch rather than a solid stitch pattern. It's easier to work into chain spaces than into stitches.

▶ Work two strands together, such as a smooth yarn along with the novelty yarn, to help distinguish the stitches.

▶ Crochet with a smooth yarn while holding the novelty yarn on the right side of the fabric. Work the stitches over the novelty yarn as you would when covering yarn tails, catching the novelty yarn in every stitch, or in every 2 or 3 stitches.

LEFT-HANDED · RIGHT-HANDED

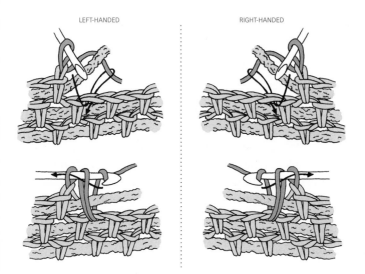

Q Do you have tips for working with slippery yarn?

A Silk, rayon ribbon, and other slick yarns are beautiful to look at, but they also present a challenge. Even if you wind them carefully, the balls have a tendency to melt into a puddle at the first opportunity. Try corralling them into a sandwich bag or

Yarn Bra

wrap them with a Yarn Bra, old pantyhose, or other stretchy material for better control.

SEE ALSO: *Pages 296–97 for weaving in slippery ends.*

Q Is there anything I can do to keep variegated yarns from appearing splotchy?

A When you get noticeable odd-shaped areas of a single color in the middle of a piece of crochet, it's known as *pooling.* Try alternating two balls of yarn or use the inside and outside ends of a single ball of yarn each row or round to avoid pooling. Or use a stitch pattern that breaks up large expanses of the variegated yarn: spike stitches, contrasting-color stripes, or texture stitches.

As the distance across the piece changes, the frequency with which certain colors show up changes. For instance, on a sweater, the yarn travels a shorter distance when you shape the armholes and neck edge than it does across the full width of the body, so the color repeats create a different pattern on these shorter rows than in the longer rows below. Therefore, you may need to use anti-pooling techniques on some parts of a garment and not on others. (Voice of Experience: You can't tell from a small swatch if your colors are going to pool.)

Q Is there any kind of yarn I can't crochet with?

A Not that I've found, although some yarns may be more challenging than others. Don't think you have to stick to "yarn," either! You can crochet with plastic bags cut into strips (*plarn*), wire, audiotape, paper, rope . . . whatever you can imagine.

Endings and Beginnings

Q How do I add a new yarn?

A There are several ways to add a new yarn, depending on the circumstances.

▶ **The traditional technique** is the same no matter what stitch you are working and whether or not you are starting a new color: Work until there are two loops left on the hook, yarnover with the new yarn and pull through both loops on hook. Then continue in the new yarn, working the next stitch or a turning chain, as appropriate.

▶ **If you don't already have a stitch on the hook,** just insert the hook into the proper spot, yarnover and pull up a loop to connect the new yarn to the existing piece. Treat this loop as you would a slip knot; you may need to chain for the height of your first stitch.

continued on next page >>

▶ **Work a standing stitch.** A third technique involves beginning a new yarn without first connecting it to the existing crocheted piece: a *standing stitch*. Read the next question and answer for more details.

No matter what technique you use to join a new yarn, always leave a tail at least 6" long on both the old and new yarns so that you can weave in the ends later.

SEE ALSO: *Page 87 for stitch heights.*

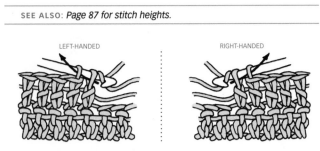

LEFT-HANDED   RIGHT-HANDED

adding a new yarn mid-row

. . . .

Q **What does it mean to "join with sc in first stitch"?**

A The most common meaning of this phrase is to begin a new yarn with a *standing single crochet*. Standing stitches are used when there is not already an existing stitch on the hook, as when the previous yarn has been fastened off. It is "standing" because the yarn starts at the top of the stitch, rather than at the bottom as with a turning chain.

Any standing stitch can be made by beginning with a slip knot on the hook. Treating the loop on the hook as you would any existing loop, work the desired stitch. For example, for a standing single crochet (or "join with sc"), begin with a slip knot on the hook, insert hook into the designated stitch or space, yarnover and pull up a loop, yarnover and pull through both loops on hook. You have completed a single crochet.

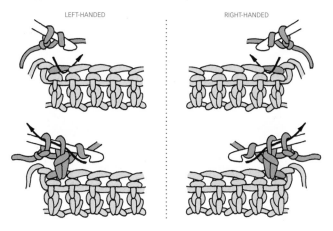

LEFT-HANDED   RIGHT-HANDED

standing single crochet

To "join with dc in first stitch" means to make a standing double crochet in the first stitch: Begin with a slip knot on the hook, holding the slip knot with your index finger to keep it from slipping, yarnover, insert the hook into the first stitch, yarnover and pull up a loop, (yarnover and pull through two loops) two times. (Another meaning of "join with dc in first st" sometimes crops up when working in the round.)

More experienced crocheters work their standing stitches by simply wrapping the yarn over the hook an extra time before starting the stitch without first putting a slip knot on the hook.

SEE ALSO: *Page 198 for joining with dc in top of turning chain.*

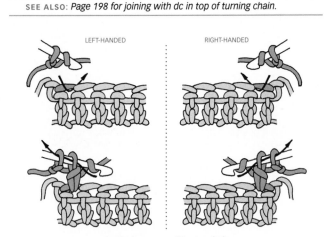

LEFT-HANDED   RIGHT-HANDED

beginning a row without a chain

CHAPTER 3

Strong Foundations

Every piece of crochet has to start somewhere. The *chain stitch* is the most basic of the crochet stitches, and a *foundation chain* serves as a base into which you work your first row of stitches.

Basic Foundation Chains

To make the foundation chain, begin with a slip knot on the hook.

. . . .

Q **How do I make a slip knot?**

A Leaving a 6-inch tail, form a loop in the yarn and hold it in your non-dominant hand with the working yarn over your index finger. Then proceed as follows:

LEFT-HANDED   RIGHT-HANDED

1. Insert hook into the center of the loop and wrap the working yarn from back to front over the hook.

2. Pull the yarn on the hook back out through the large center loop.

3. Tug gently on the working yarn to snug the knot around the hook.

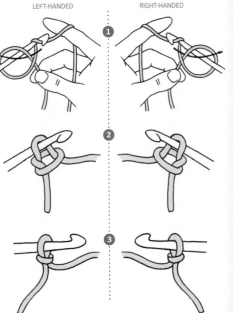

Q How do I make the foundation chain?

A Begin with a slip knot on the hook as described in the previous question, then proceed as follows:

chain stitch symbol

1. Wrap the yarn around the hook from back to front and draw the working yarn through the slip knot (first chain stitch made).

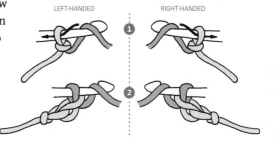

LEFT-HANDED RIGHT-HANDED

2. Continue to wrap the yarn over the hook (this is called a *yarnover* [yo]) and to pull it through the loop on the hook for each subsequent chain stitch.

Q Does it really matter which way I wrap the yarn over the hook?

A Yes, always wrap the yarn over the hook from back to front. Try thinking of it this way: If the working yarn is over your forefinger and behind the hook, push back with the hook, then bring the yarn down with your finger in front of the hook; the yarn will be wrapped over the hook in the right direction.

Q What should I do if I'm having trouble getting the loop on my hook over the head of the hook?

A First, make sure that you are wrapping the yarn over the hook in the right direction. If your yarnover is correct, the problem might be the slip knot: Make sure that your slip knot isn't too tight. If the problem is subsequent stitches, be sure that you aren't holding the yarn too tightly whenever you are making a stitch. The following technique may also help:

1. When making the yarnover, the head of the hook should be facing you.

2. As you pull the yarn through the loop on the hook, rotate the hook head 90 degrees so that it faces down toward the chain.

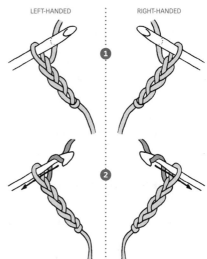

LEFT-HANDED

RIGHT-HANDED

rotating the hook to draw the yarn through

Q How do I keep the growing foundation chain under control?

A With the working yarn over the forefinger of your non-dominant hand, hold the piece that you are stitching with your thumb and middle finger of that same hand near the hook. As the chain gets longer, keep moving your fingers up close to the hook. This leaves your dominant hand free to maneuver the hook.

Q How do I make an even chain?

A Chaining evenly takes a bit of practice. When you're just starting to learn to crochet, it may take a while before you are comfortable holding the yarn and hook. Try not to be discouraged! Concentrate on working loosely and evenly, and practice keeping the fingers that are holding the yarn close to the hook. Make sure to form your stitches on the shank of the hook and not on the narrower throat. Remember to relax your shoulders and *breathe*.

SEE ALSO: *Page 14 for parts of the crochet hook.*

Q How will I know if my foundation chain is the correct tension?

A Do your stitches look consistent? All the stitches should look almost the same size. Are you easily able to work your first row into the chain? After you have worked the foundation chain and the first row or two of your piece, lay it flat on a table and look at it critically. Do the stitches in the next rows flare above the foundation chain? If so, you need a looser chain. Do the stitches pull in above the foundation? If so, you need a tighter foundation chain. In either case, start over from scratch to make the appropriate adjustments. (Voice of Experience: You'll save time and effort if you make these adjustments while you're still working on your sample swatch and don't wait until the actual project.)

SEE ALSO: *Pages 155–69 for swatches.*

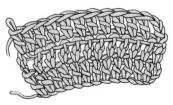

too tight a foundation chain

too loose a foundation chain

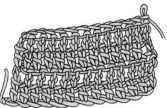

Q How do I fix a foundation chain that's too tight?

A Unfortunately, there is no good fix for a too-tight foundation chain, so it's important to get it right from the beginning. If you notice right away that your chain is too tight, rip it out and start over. Many people tend to tighten up when working chain stitches. You may find it helps to use a larger hook for the foundation chain, and then switch on the first row or round to the size you need to get the correct gauge. You may prefer to use a foundation single crochet or other foundation stitch in place of a foundation chain.

SEE ALSO: *Pages 80–82 for foundation chain variations.*

Q How do I count chains?

A This question confounds many crocheters. Hold your chain so that it is not twisted; you should see a stack

counting the chains

of Vs facing you. Count each V as a stitch, but don't count the slip knot or the loop on the hook.

Some crocheters find that it makes counting easier if they insert a marker every 10 or 20 stitches when making a long chain.

continued on next page >>

It's also a good idea to chain a few too many when working a long chain. That way, if you missed your count by a few stitches, you don't have to start over. You can pick out any extra chains later.

markers in foundation chain

picking out extra chains

Q How long does my foundation chain have to be?

A If you are following a published pattern, the instructions tell you. Sometimes the instructions say to work a "multiple of 4 plus 2." This means that your stitch pattern requires any multiple of 4 stitches plus 2 for turning or to balance a stitch pattern (for instance, a total of 6, 10, 14, or more chains).

SEE ALSO: *Page 150 for multiples.*

If you are working without a published pattern, chain as many stitches as you need for the number of stitches on the first row, plus the number you need for a turning chain. The number of stitches in a turning chain is based on the height of the first stitch you'll work on the first row (see Starting the First Row, page 79).

SEE ALSO: *Page 87 for height of stitches.*

Q Where in the stitch do I insert my hook into a foundation chain?

A Take a moment to look at the construction of the chain. The front of the chain looks like a row of sideways Vs; the back of the chain has a row of bumps. You have several choices about where to insert your hook on the first row. You may choose to insert your hook just above the bottom loop, under both the top loop of the V and the bump. Sometimes this is described as the "top two loops" of the chain.

Another excellent option is to turn the chain over and insert your hook under each of the bumps (or "humps") on the back of the chain. The advantage of this method is that it leaves a smooth chained edge at the bottom of your piece. However, if your yarn makes either of those methods difficult, or if you are unhappy with the way your first row looks, try inserting the hook into just the top loop of the chain. No matter which method you use, choose one and be consistent across the row.

working under top two loops on front of chain

working in back bumps

Q Which of the stitches in the foundation chain should I start with?

A Which stitch you insert the hook into first depends on what type of stitch you are working on the first row, and whether the turning portion of the chain is going to count as a stitch. The taller the stitch, the further back along the chain you insert the hook.

Q How can I make the bottom corner of my crochet more square? One corner always seems to be more rounded than the other.

A Make sure you are using the appropriate number of extra chains for your first turning chain (see the chart at right). You could also try making your turning chains (the last few chains of your foundation chain) slightly looser.

Q How can I tell if my foundation chain is twisted?

A The chain should look like a little row of stacked Vs from the front side. If it doesn't, you twisted your chain. Rip back to the place where it was twisted and rework.

Starting the First Row

FIRST STITCH OF FIRST ROW	EXTRA STITCHES IN FOUNDATION CHAIN if turning chain does *not* count as a stitch	EXTRA STITCHES IN FOUNDATION CHAIN if turning chain *does* count as a stitch	CHAINS FROM HOOK FOR FIRST STITCH
Slip stitch	1		2nd
Single crochet	1		2nd
Half double crochet	2	1	3rd
Double crochet	3	2	4th
Treble/ Triple crochet	4	3	5th

SEE ALSO: *Page 105 for turning chains; pages 91–104 for single, double, half double, treble crochet, and slip stitch.*

Variations on Foundation Chains

Q **Do I always have to work a foundation chain?**

A Not always. Although you always need some sort of base into which to work the first row or round of stitches, there is an option other than a foundation chain. You can combine the foundation chain and first row of the stitching into a single step. These chainless foundations create an elastic edge and may prevent a too-tight foundation chain. They are often used in place of a chain and a single row of stitches, as for a cord, or for increasing many stitches at the edge of a piece. However, because they do not look exactly like a standard "foundation chain plus Row 1," the two methods should probably not be mixed within the same project. Here's how to make both foundation single crochet (fsc) and foundation double crochet (fdc):

MAKING A SINGLE CROCHET FOUNDATION

1. Beginning with a slip knot on the hook, ch 2, insert hook in 2nd chain from hook.

2. Yarnover and pull up a loop, yarnover and pull through 1 loop — *(1 chain made)*.

3. Yarnover and pull through two loops — *(1 fsc made)*. For each subsequent fsc, insert the hook into the chain at the base of the previous fsc, and repeat steps 2 and 3 for the desired number of stitches.

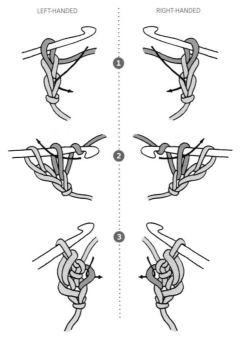

LEFT-HANDED · RIGHT-HANDED

MAKING A DOUBLE CROCHET FOUNDATION

1. Beginning with a slip knot on the hook, ch 4, yarnover, insert hook in 4th chain from hook. Yarnover and pull up a loop, yarnover and pull through one loop — *(1 chain made)*.

2 and 3. (Yarnover and pull through two loops) two times — *(1 fdc made)*.

3. For each subsequent fdc, insert the hook into the chain at the base of the previous fdc, and repeat steps 2 and 3 for the desired number of stitches.

LEFT-HANDED   RIGHT-HANDED

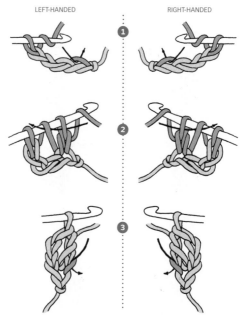

Q My instructions say to "work on opposite side of chain." What does that mean?

A Sometimes it's necessary to stitch into both sides of the foundation chain; for instance, when you are making an oval or starting a three-dimensional piece. Typically, you start by working a row into the foundation chain in the usual way, inserting your hook into the top two loops as described earlier. If you want a rounded end, work several stitches into the last stitch of the foundation chain, then rotate the chain so that the front is still facing you but the bottom of the chain is now on top. Continue to work stitches into the remaining unworked loops on the other side of the chain, placing several stitches into the last stitch to match the other end. Join with a slip stitch to the first stitch.

SEE ALSO: *Pages 190–92 for stitching an oval.*

If you want a square end rather than a rounded end, cut the yarn and fasten off after working the first row across the foundation chain. Turn the piece so that the row you just worked is on the bottom and the remaining loops of the foundation chain are on top. With right side facing, rejoin the yarn at the right-hand corner (*or the left-hand corner for Lefties*) and stitch into each loop on the other side of the chain. You may also work into the opposite side of the chain when you add on an edging.

SEE ALSO: *Chapter 10, On the Edge*

Q How can I get the beginning and ending of my piece to look the same?

A When you work the first row, if you insert your hook into just the bumps on the back of the chain, the beginning and ending will match: a tidy row of Vs marching along the top and bottom edges.

CHAPTER 4

In Stitches

The word *stitch* in crochet sometimes refers to the most familiar stitch patterns, such as single and double crochet, or it may be used to indicate variations of the basics like popcorn and shells. In this chapter, we'll talk about all of these.

The Basic Stitches

Q How are stitches formed?

A At its most basic, crochet is just a series of loops. Every crochet stitch pattern, no matter how complex, is made up of only three basic movements, all involving loops:

1. Wrap yarn around hook (yarnover).
2. Insert hook somewhere.
3. Pull yarn through something.

The combination of these three steps, the order in which they are accomplished, and the placement of the hook makes for the endless variety of crocheted stitch patterns available to us.

. . . .

Q What is a *stitch pattern*?

A A stitch pattern is a specific combination of stitches that, when repeated, creates a crocheted fabric. Sometimes just the word *stitch* is used as a shortcut for the phrase.

Q What are the most common stitches?

A The most common stitches are chain (ch), single crochet (sc), and double crochet (dc). Slip stitch (sl st), half double crochet (hdc), and treble crochet (tr) are also commonly used, even in simple designs.

Q How do I make the most common stitches?

A As mentioned, all crochet stitches are made using a similar series of movements. The shorter stitches require fewer steps than the taller stitches. On the following pages, you can find step-by-step illustrations of how to make each stitch. When you need at-a-glance information, go to the table on pages 88 and 89 for a quick reference (as well as a comparison) of what's involved for each stitch.

Q What does *stitch height* mean?

A With the exception of slip stitch, all crocheted stitches have height, ranging from the short single crochet, up to and beyond the tall treble crochet. Becoming familiar with the relative height of each stitch helps you understand how long each turning chain must be. It is also useful when shaping curves in a piece.

Stitches at a Glance*

		STEP 1	STEP 2	STEP 3
CHAIN STITCH	⊖	Yarnover	Pull yarn through loop on hook	
SLIP STITCH	•	Insert hook into stitch(es) or space(es) indicated	Yarnover	Pull yarn through everything on hook
SINGLE CROCHET	+ OR ×	Insert hook into stitch or space indicated	Yarnover	Pull yarn up through stitch or space (2 loops on hook)
HALF DOUBLE CROCHET	T	Yarnover	Insert hook into stitch or space indicated	Pull yarn up through stitch or space (3 loops on hook)
DOUBLE CROCHET	T	Yarnover	Insert hook into stitch or space indicated	Pull yarn up through stitch or space (3 loops on hook)
TREBLE (TRIPLE) CROCHET	T	Yarnover twice	Insert hook into stitch or space indicated	Pull yarn up through stitch or space (4 loops on hook)

*U.S. terminology

SEE ALSO: *Page 113 for U.S. versus UK terminology.*

STEP 4	STEP 5	STEPS 6–7	STEPS 8–9
Yarnover	Pull yarn through both loops on hook		
Yarnover	Pull yarn through 3 loops on hook		
Yarnover	Pull yarn through 2 loops on hook	Repeat Steps 4 and 5	
Yarnover	Pull yarn through 2 loops on hook	Repeat Steps 4 and 5	Repeat Steps 4 and 5

Q What are the stitches in order of height?

A The basic stitch patterns, in order of height, are:

Chain stitch
Slip stitch
Single crochet
Half double crochet
Double crochet
Treble crochet

There are also some extended stitches that fall in between the basic stitches heightwise. A more complete list is:

Chain stitch (ch)
Slip stitch (sl st)
Single crochet (sc)
Extended single crochet (esc)
Half double crochet (hdc)
Extended half double crochet (ehdc)
Double crochet (dc)
Extended double crochet (edc)
Treble crochet (tr)
Extended treble crochet (etr)
Double treble crochet (dtr), and so on

Q How do I make a single crochet stitch?

A The illustrations on pages 91 and 92 show how to make a single crochet into a chain and into a foundation row.

+ or ✗
single crochet symbol

SINGLE CROCHET INTO A CHAIN

1. Insert the hook into the second chain from the hook, wrap the yarn over the hook (called *yarnover*, and abbreviated *yo*), pull up a loop. Now you have two loops on your hook.

2. Wrap the yarn over the hook again and pull it through both loops on the hook to complete the first single crochet.

3. Continue working into the foundation chain all the way back to the slip knot, but don't work into the slip knot. Count to make sure you have the number of stitches you are supposed to have.

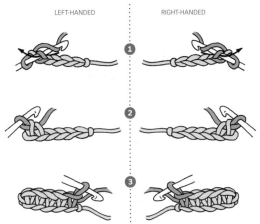

LEFT-HANDED · RIGHT-HANDED

SINGLE CROCHET INTO AN ESTABLISHED ROW

1. Chain 1 to make a turning chain and get your hook up to the level of the single crochet stitch.

2. Turn the crochet as you would turn the page of a book, so that you can work the next row from right to left (*left to right for Lefties*). Insert the hook under both loops at the

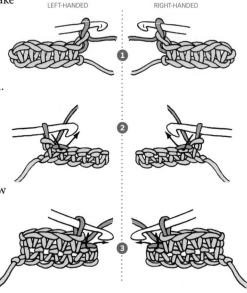

LEFT-HANDED   RIGHT-HANDED

top of the last stitch in the previous row. (This is the stitch below the chain-1.)

3. Yarnover and pull up a loop, then yarnover and pull through two loops (as in steps 1 and 2 for single crochet above). Continue across the row, working into both loops of each stitch across.

Be sure to work into the last stitch, then count again to make sure you still have the same number of stitches.

Q How do I make a half double crochet stitch?

A The steps below show how to make a
half double crochet into a chain, as well
as into an already-established foundation row.

half double
crochet
symbol

HALF DOUBLE CROCHET INTO A CHAIN

1. Wrap the yarn over the hook, then insert the hook into
the third chain from the hook. Yarnover and pull up a loop.
You have three loops on your hook.

2. Wrap the yarn over the hook again and pull it through all
three loops on the hook to complete the half double crochet.

3. Continue working into the foundation chain all the way
back to the slip knot, but don't work into the slip knot. Count
to make sure you have the number of stitches you are supposed

LEFT-HANDED   RIGHT-HANDED

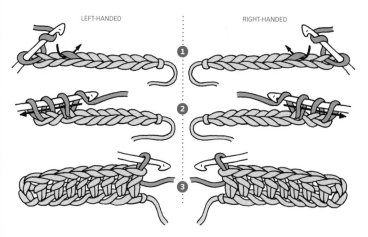

to have. This example counts the two chains you skipped at the beginning of the row as a stitch.

HALF DOUBLE CROCHET INTO AN ESTABLISHED ROW

1. Chain 2 to make a turning chain, and get your hook up to the level of the half double crochet stitch. Turn the crochet as you would turn the page of a book, so that you can work the next row from right to left (*left to right for Lefties*).

2. Yarnover and insert hook under both loops at the top of the next-to-last stitch in the previous row. Note that you are skipping the very first stitch at the base of the chain, because in this example the turning chain counts as the first stitch.

LEFT-HANDED   RIGHT-HANDED

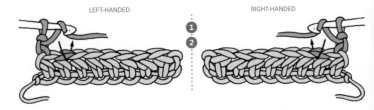

3. Yarnover and pull up a loop, yarnover and pull through all three loops to complete the half double crochet. Continue across the row, working into both loops of each stitch across. Since this example counts the chain-2 turning chain as a stitch, work the last stitch into the top of the chain-2 turning chain from the previous row. Count again to make sure you still have the same number of stitches, counting the beginning chain-2 as a stitch.

SEE ALSO: *Page 105 for turning chains.*

LEFT-HANDED

RIGHT-HANDED

Q How do I make a double crochet stitch?

A The steps below show how to make a double crochet into a chain as well as into an established foundation row.

double crochet symbol

DOUBLE CROCHET INTO A CHAIN

1. Wrap the yarn over the hook, then insert the hook into the fourth chain from the hook. Yarnover and pull up a loop. You have three loops on your hook.

2. Yarnover again and pull it through the first two loops on the hook. Two loops remain on the hook.

3. Yarnover again and pull through both loops on the hook to complete the double crochet.

4. Continue working into the foundation chain all the way back to the slip knot, but don't work into the slip knot. Count to make sure you have the number of stitches you are supposed to have. Count the three chains you skipped at the beginning of the row as a stitch.

LEFT-HANDED

RIGHT-HANDED

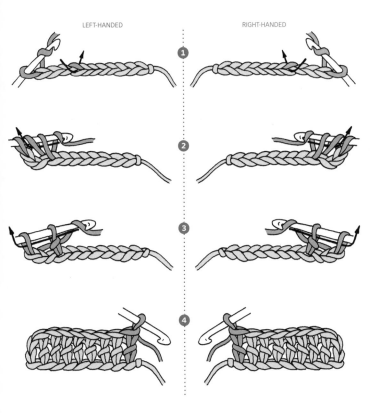

DOUBLE CROCHET INTO AN ESTABLISHED ROW

1. Chain 3 to make a turning chain and get your hook up to the level of the double crochet stitch. Turn the crochet as you would turn the page of a book, so that you can work the next row from right to left (*left to right for Lefties*).

2. Yarnover and insert hook under both loops at the top of the next-to-last stitch in the previous row. Note that you are skipping the very first stitch at the base of the chain, because the turning chain counts as the first stitch.

3. Yarnover and pull up a loop, yarnover and pull through two loops, then yarnover and pull through the remaining two loops to complete the double crochet. Continue across the row, working into both loops of each stitch across. Work the last stitch into the top of the chain-3 turning chain from the previous row. Count again to make sure you still have the same number of stitches, counting the beginning chain-3 as a stitch.

LEFT-HANDED

RIGHT-HANDED

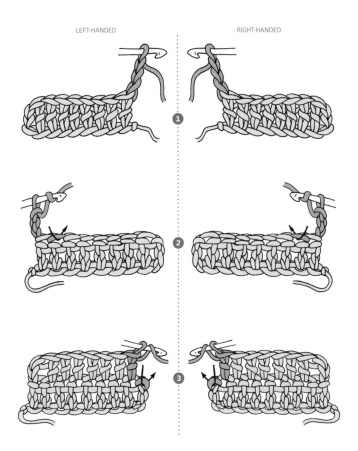

Q How do I make a treble crochet stitch?

A The steps below show how to make a treble crochet into a chain as well as into an established foundation row.

treble crochet symbol

TREBLE CROCHET INTO A CHAIN

1. Wrap the yarn over the hook two times, then insert the hook into the fifth chain from the hook.

2. Yarnover and pull up a loop. You have four loops on your hook.

3. Yarnover and pull through the first two loops on the hook, leaving three loops on the hook.

4. Yarnover again and pull through two loops. You now have two loops on the hook.

5. One more "yarnover and pull through two loops" leaves you with a single loop on the hook and a completed treble crochet.

6. Continue working into the foundation chain all the way back to the slip knot, but don't work into the slip knot. Count to make sure you have the number of stitches you are supposed to have. Count the four chains you skipped at the beginning of the row as a stitch.

LEFT-HANDED   RIGHT-HANDED

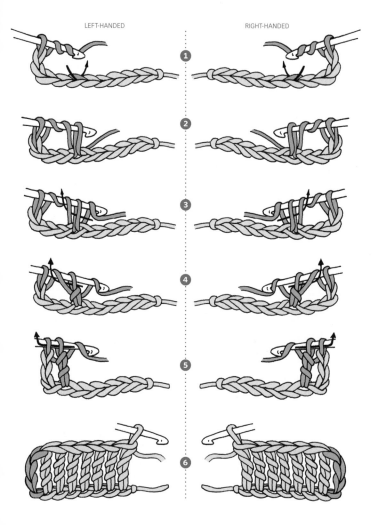

TREBLE CROCHET INTO AN
ESTABLISHED ROW

1. Chain 4 to make a turning chain and get your hook up to the level of the treble crochet stitch. Turn the crochet as you would turn the page of a book, so that you can work the next row from right to left (*left to right for Lefties*).

2. Yarnover two times and insert hook under both loops at the top of the next-to-last stitch in the previous row. Note that you are skipping the very first stitch at the base of the chain, because the turning chain counts as the first stitch. Work steps 2–5 as for Treble Crochet into a Chain above.

LEFT-HANDED   RIGHT-HANDED

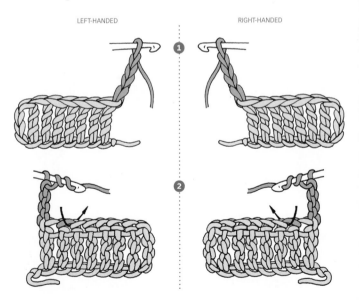

LEFT-HANDED RIGHT-HANDED

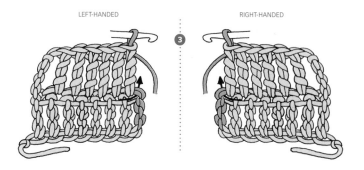

3. Continue across the row, working into both loops of each stitch across. Work the last stitch into the top of the turning chain from the previous row. Count again to make sure you still have the same number of stitches, counting the beginning chain-4 as a stitch.

....

Q **What is the difference between *treble crochet* and *triple crochet*?**

A The way they are spelled and pronounced! They are the same thing. "Treble" used to be more commonly considered a British term but is becoming the preferred American term as well. In this book, we use the term treble instead of triple.

Q **How do I make a slip stitch?**

A The slip stitch (often abbreviated *sl st*) is the most basic stitch beyond the chain. Simply insert your hook into the designated stitch or space, yarnover and pull the yarn through everything on the hook.

•

slip stitch symbol

Placing the Hook and Turning Chains

Q **What does it mean to "insert hook in next stitch"?**

A The top of each stitch looks like a sideways V or chain. When you work back and forth in rows, the V lies slightly to the left of the next stitch (*or to the right, for Lefties*) that you made in the previous row. When you work in rounds, the V lies slightly to the right (left) of the next stitch that you made in the previous round. Insert the hook under both legs of this V unless your pattern instructions say otherwise.

Q **What is the difference between working into a chain space or into a chain stitch, and how do I know which to do?**

A Working into a chain space means inserting the hook into the space formed by one or more chain stitches, while working into a chain stitch means inserting the hook directly into the individual stitches of the chain itself. Most patterns expect any stitches that appear over a chain to be worked into the chain space rather than into individual chain stitches, but there are exceptions. Assume that you should work into the space unless the pattern specifies otherwise. To work into the space, insert the hook under the entire chain stitch and pull up a loop from around the other side of the chain.

LEFT-HANDED   RIGHT-HANDED

working into a space

Q **What is a *turning chain*?**

A A turning chain is the little chain worked at the beginning of a row to bring the hook up to the level of the stitches to be formed on the next row. Some patterns include the turning chain at the end of a row; many newer patterns include these instructions at the beginning of the next row, as the turning chain often acts as the first stitch in the next row. Either method accomplishes the same goal.

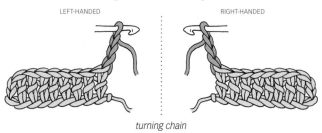

LEFT-HANDED   RIGHT-HANDED

turning chain

Q Why did I work into the last stitch on the previous row for single crochet, but the next-to-last stitch on the previous row for the other stitches?

A In single crochet, the chain-1 turning chain does not count as a stitch, so you had to work a stitch into that same spot. In taller stitches, it is common to count the turning chain as a stitch, although you should always refer to your pattern for clarification of whether the turning chain counts as a stitch. When a turning chain counts as a stitch, if you worked your first real stitch into the same stitch as the chain, you would be increasing a stitch, so you must work the first stitch into the second stitch (the next-to-last stitch from the previous row).

Q Where do I insert my hook into a stitch at the beginning of a row?

A The answer depends on whether you are counting a turning chain as a stitch. If the turning chain at the beginning of the row is not going to count as a stitch, insert the hook into the base of the turning chain. If the turning chain is going to count as a stitch, skip the base of the turning chain and insert the hook into the first sideways V that you see.

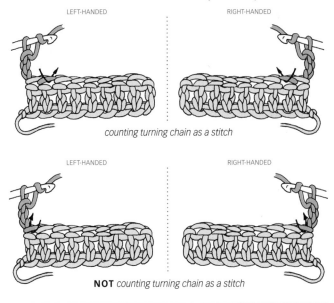

LEFT-HANDED   RIGHT-HANDED

counting turning chain as a stitch

LEFT-HANDED   RIGHT-HANDED

NOT *counting turning chain as a stitch*

SEE ALSO: *Page 197, Where do I put my hook when working in rounds?*

Q How do I know if the turning chain should be counted as a stitch?

A If you are following a published pattern, the instructions should tell you. For example, the second row of the pattern might read:

Row 2: Ch 3 (counts as dc), dc in each dc to end.

The "counts as dc" means that this chain-3 turning chain (abbreviated *ch-3*) is meant to be counted as a stitch, so you should work into the top of it on the next row as if it were a regular double crochet. Subsequent pattern rows may not state "counts as dc," but you are meant to assume that all ch-3 turning chains count as a double crochet for this pattern unless the instructions say otherwise.

If you are designing your own pattern, you may choose whether or not to regard the turning chain as a stitch. Most of the time, in double crochet and taller stitches, you do count the turning chain as a stitch. Half double crochet can go either way; just be consistent. Some stitch patterns are easier to work if the turning chain is not part of the pattern.

Single crochet turning chains are short and often hard to find or work into, so it is usually used as an aid to reach the top of the new row, but not as a stitch.

No matter which method you use — counting a turning chain as a stitch or not — you should be consistent within your project. If you aren't consistent, you'll have difficulty maintaining the correct number of stitches across the row, resulting in uneven edges.

Q How can I recognize a turning chain?

A It won't look quite like the other stitches. In fact, it may be a bit tricky to recognize where the "top" of the turning chain is. The regular stitches have nice tidy Vs at their top; a turning chain does not. Try this tip to make it easier to

LEFT-HANDED   RIGHT-HANDED

*placing a stitch marker in
last chain of turning chain*

locate the top of the turning chain when you reach it on the next row: Work the chain, then take the hook out and insert it from the other direction, instead of twisting the chain. Or you might find it helpful to put a stitch marker in the last chain of your turning chain, so that you can then work into the marked stitch on the return row.

. . . .

Q How do I know whether or not to work a stitch into the turning chain from the previous row?

A If a turning chain counts as a stitch on one row, you treat it as a stitch and work a stitch into it on the next row.

. . . .

Q When I use a turning chain, I'm not happy with the way it looks. Can I begin a row without a turning chain?

A Sometimes the turning chain just looks too flimsy next to the other stitches in the row, or leaves an unattractive hole where you would like to have a more solid stitch. Here are some other ideas:

▶ **If you are beginning a new color,** or are starting the new row in a different spot, just use a standing stitch (see page 67) to begin the new row.

▶ **On the taller stitches,** try using 1 chain fewer; sometimes a ch-2 turning chain for double crochet is sufficient.

▶ **Ignore the turning chain,** and work the first stitch of the row into the stitch at the base of the chain. In other words, don't use the turning chain as a stitch.

▶ **Instead of using a turning chain at all,** simply pull the first loop on the hook up to the level of your next row and begin stitching in the first stitch. In these last two methods, the turning-chain-that's-not-a-stitch and the long-loop-that's-not-a-stitch simply get covered by the edging or incorporated into a seam at finishing time.

SEE ALSO: *Page 67 for standing stitches.*

Working with Basic Stitches

Q **What does it mean when the directions say to "sc into each sc" or "dc into each sc"?**

A This is just a reminder of the nature of the stitch pattern in the previous row, combined with instructions about what to do in the current row. Knowing that you are making a single crochet row over a previous row of single crochet (in the first instance) or a row of double crochet over a row of single crochet (in the second instance) assures you that you are working the stitch pattern as intended.

SEE ALSO: *Chapter 7, A Whole Cloth for more on fabric.*

Q My stitches don't look like the ones in the picture. Why not?

A There are several possibilities:

▶ You may be having a problem with American/British terms. If you are reading a British pattern, you'll have to "translate" the pattern into American stitches to achieve the right look. (And vice versa, of course.)

▶ Sometimes you must work several rows before you can see a stitch pattern develop. Stitch patterns with multiple row repeats may require a complete repeat or two before the pattern is apparent.

▶ Recheck the pattern instructions to see if there are any special instructions you missed. If you think you are following the instructions correctly, it may pay to continue for another few rows to see what develops.

▶ The pattern might be wrong. Despite designers' and publishers' best efforts, errors do creep into patterns.

SEE ALSO: *Chapter 8, Pattern Language and Symbols for pattern reading; page 113 for U.S. and UK terms.*

Q What's the difference between American and British pattern instructions?

A Whoever said that the United States and the United Kingdom are two countries divided by a single language might have been thinking of crocheters, because

crochet terminology differs significantly between the two countries. Yarn descriptions and hook sizing may be different, as well. We use American terms throughout this book, but you need to be aware of the differences when reading a British pattern.

SEE ALSO: *Pages 42–43 for hook and yarn information.*

One Language, Two Meanings

U.S. TERM	UK TERM
Slip stitch	Slip stitch
Single crochet	Double crochet
Half double crochet	Half treble crochet
Double crochet	Treble crochet
Treble/triple crochet	Double treble crochet
Double treble crochet	Treble treble crochet
Yarnover	Yarn over hook
Gauge	Tension

Q **What are some uses for slip stitch?**

A The slip stitch is most often used for joining rounds, for seaming, and for moving the yarn and hook to a different spot without adding height to a row. For example, when you are decreasing for an armhole, you might use a slip stitch to move the yarn and hook in from the edge of the fabric without building height. It is used for creating some specialty stitch patterns, as well.

SEE ALSO: *Page 104 for slip stitch.*

Q What are some uses for chain stitch?

A The versatile chain stitch is ideal for shoelaces, ties, drawstrings, handles, buttonholes, turning chains, foundation chains, decorative increases, and lacy stitch patterns. In stitch patterns, it is used in conjunction with other stitches to create open spaces.

SEE ALSO: *Page 71 for chain stitch.*

Q What does it mean to "pull up a loop"?

A This is the basic move in every crochet stitch. It means to wrap the yarn around the hook and pull it through the fabric. It is usually preceded by "insert hook into stitch/ fabric/etc., yarnover, and . . ."

Q What does *end off* or *fasten off* mean?

A This is what you do to secure the last stitch and keep it from unraveling. Take your hook out of the stitch and cut the yarn, leaving at least a 6" tail. Pull this end through the last stitch and pull it tight.

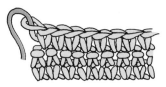

fastening off

. . . .

Q Do I have to put my hook into the top of the next stitch as I crochet?

A Certainly not! Exploring new territory with your hook makes crochet endlessly intriguing. There are many places you can put your hook other than into the "next stitch." Once you're familiar with the basic stitch patterns, you can go on to explore those other places. Here are a few options:

▶ Work into just the front or just the back loop of the next stitch.

▶ Skip stitches, work between stitches, around posts (see page 117), in spaces, in rows below, or into the sides of existing stitches.

▶ Work into previous stitches on the same row or into stitches on previous rows.

▶ Take your hook out of your work and insert it into a different spot altogether!

Q Where do I put my hook when it says "back loop only" or "front loop only"?

A The *back loop* of a stitch is the one that is farther away as you look at the work. The *front loop* is the one closer to you. Inserting into one or the other gives a completely different look to the stitch.

˘

front loop symbol

◠

back loop symbol

SEE ALSO: *Page 197 for Where do I put my hook when working in rounds?*

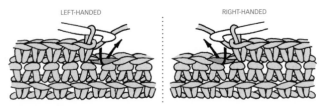

LEFT-HANDED   RIGHT-HANDED

single crochet in front loop

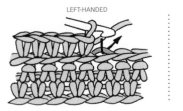 

LEFT-HANDED   RIGHT-HANDED

single crochet in back loop

Q What is a *post*?

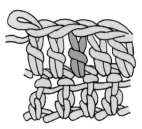

double crochet post

A The post is the vertical part of the stitch. Single crochet stitches have a post, but they are hard to find! For that reason, many front post and back post stitches are worked into double crochet and taller stitches.

Q What is *front post double crochet* and *back post double crochet*?

A These stitches are created by putting your hook around the post of the next stitch on the previous row instead of into the top loop. Often crocheting around the post is alternated with single crochet.

▶ **For front post double crochet (FPdc).** Yarnover; keeping hook in front of work, insert hook from front to back to front around post of next stitch and pull up a loop; *yarnover, pull through two loops on hook; repeat from * once.

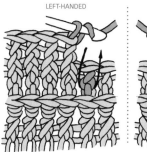

LEFT-HANDED · RIGHT-HANDED

front post double crochet symbol

117

▶ **For back post double crochet (BPdc).** Yarnover; keeping hook in back of work, insert hook from back to front to back around post of next stitch and pull up a loop; *yarnover, pull through two loops on hook; repeat from * once.

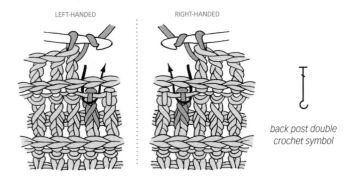

LEFT-HANDED   RIGHT-HANDED

back post double crochet symbol

. . . .

Q **Do I need to adjust my turning chain for front post and back post double crochet?**

A Because working around the post brings the new stitch down into the previous row, it creates a shorter-than-normal height for the row. You may need to chain only one or two stitches to reach the needed height for your next row. If you are alternating front/back post double crochet with single crochet stitches, just chain 1.

Q How do I put my hook between stitches?

A Instead of inserting the hook under the top V of the stitch, insert it in between the posts of the stitches on the previous row. This creates a more open fabric (and a different gauge) than stitching into the tops of the stitches.

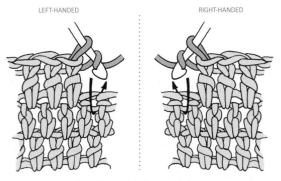

LEFT-HANDED   RIGHT-HANDED

inserting hook between stitches

Q What is the *row below*?

A Sometimes, instructions tell you to work into a stitch in "the row below" or "two rows below," rather than into the top of the next stitch. This can be confusing, because you are already working into the row below your current row. However, in this case the instruction probably means to work into the next-to-last row you completed — in other words, the *row below* the row you would ordinarily work into. Therefore, "two rows below" would mean to work into the stitch that is two rows below the stitch you would ordinarily work into. With any luck, there will be a symbol crochet chart to help you understand where to put your stitches!

Sometimes stitches worked into one or more "rows below" are called *spike stitches*. These "spike" down into the fabric, partially covering previous stitches. A spike stitch will produce a spike on the front and the back of the fabric.

LEFT-HANDED   RIGHT-HANDED

working single crochet into the row below

Q How do I count stitches?

A Take a close look at your work and learn to recognize how each stitch is made:

▶ **For the row you just worked.** The top of each stitch looks like a sideways V, so if you count the Vs, you are counting stitches. Do not count the loop on the hook as a stitch.

▶ **For previous rows.** Count each bump of a single crochet or each post of a double or treble crochet, plus the turning chain (if your pattern directed that it be counted as a stitch).

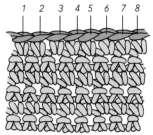

counting single crochets in current row

▶ **For highly textured yarn.** You may have to count stitches as you work them or use your fingers to feel and count the bumps. (Each bump is a stitch.)

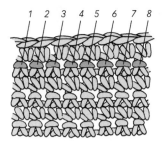

counting single crochets in previous rows

Q How do I count rows?

A As you get familiar with the look of the various stitches, this will get easier for you.

▶ **For back-and-forth single crochet.** Look for the distinct line between each pair of rows.

▶ **For in-the-round single crochet.** Look for the distinct line between each round.

▶ **For double and treble crochet.** Count each row or round of posts.

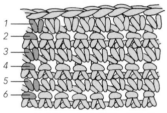

counting rows in back and forth single crochet

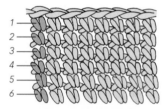

counting rounds in single crochet

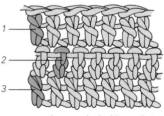

counting rows in double crochet

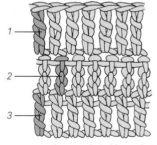

counting rows in treble crochet

Q How do I work into a slip stitch?

A First, be sure that you are indeed supposed to work into it. Most commonly, slip stitches are used to move the yarn inconspicuously to a different spot in the work without intending to work into the stitch at a later time. Other times, slip stitch is meant to join rounds. In either case, you are not meant to work into the slip stitch. If you are certain that you are supposed to work into the stitch, take care to work loosely enough when making the slip stitch so that you are able to insert the hook into the stitch on the next row or round.

Q My stitches are so tight I have trouble getting the hook into them on the next row. Can you help?

A It shouldn't be difficult to put the hook into the stitches. If you are struggling to maneuver your hook, consider the following:

▶ Is the size of your hook appropriate for the yarn or thread you are using?

▶ Are you keeping too much tension on the yarn? Some crocheters use a tight tension in an effort to make their stitches even. Not a good idea!

▶ Is there tension on the yarn between the ball and your hand? Pull out some extra yarn so that the only tension comes between your yarn hand and the hook. Concentrate on allowing the yarn to flow through your fingers.

continued on next page >>

▶ Are you making the stitch on the throat of the hook instead of on the shank? Make sure your loop finds the full diameter of the hook before you begin the next stitch. You may find it easier to use a hook with an inline head and a straight shank.

Decreasing and Increasing

Q How do I decrease a stitch?

A The easiest way to decrease is simply to skip a stitch. However, this may make an unsightly hole in the fabric. In general, the best way to decrease is to work the stitch until just before the last step — the last "yarnover and pull through." Work the next stitch in the same manner, then yarnover and pull through all the loops on the hook. Study the illustrations on the following pages for what that means for the single, half double, and double crochet:

SINGLE CROCHET DECREASE (SC DEC OR SC2TOG)

1. (Insert hook in next stitch, pull up loop) two times.
2. Yarnover and pull through three loops on hook.

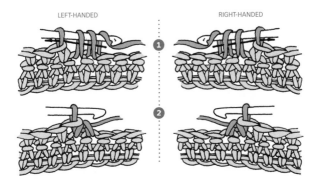

LEFT-HANDED   RIGHT-HANDED

HALF DOUBLE CROCHET DECREASE (HDC DEC OR HDC2TOG)

1. (Yarnover, insert hook in next stitch and pull up loop) two times.

2. Yarnover and pull through five loops on hook.

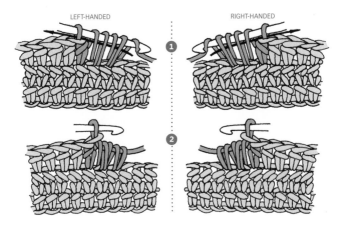

LEFT-HANDED   RIGHT-HANDED

DOUBLE CROCHET DECREASE (DC DEC OR DC2TOG)

1. (Yarnover, insert hook in next stitch, pull up loop, yarnover and pull through two loops on hook) two times.

2. Yarnover and pull through three loops on hook.

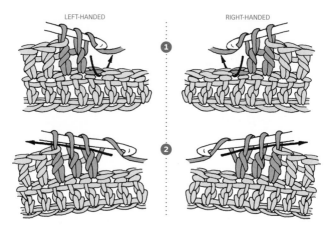

LEFT-HANDED

RIGHT-HANDED

Q Are there more refined ways to decrease?

A Yes, indeed. Experiment with the following alternate decrease methods, which may offer a less obtrusive look to fit your needs.

ALTERNATE DECREASE 1

▶ **On right side rows, for single crochet,** insert hook into next stitch from front to back, then into second stitch from back to front, yarnover and pull up a loop through both stitches, yarnover and pull through both loops on hook. Try the same decrease using the front loops only.

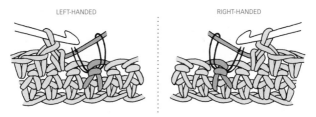

LEFT-HANDED   RIGHT-HANDED

alternate decrease 1 (sc)

▶ **On wrong side rows, for single crochet,** insert hook into next stitch from back to front, then into second stitch from front to back, yarnover and pull up a loop through both stitches, yarnover and pull through both loops on hook.

▶ **For half double and double crochet.** Work as for the single crochet decrease, but yarnover once before inserting the hook into the first stitch, then work the loops off the hook as needed for the stitch you are creating.

ALTERNATE DECREASE 2

▶ **For single crochet,** insert hook into next stitch, yarnover and pull up a loop, insert hook into next stitch, yarnover and pull through all loops on hook.

LEFT-HANDED   RIGHT-HANDED

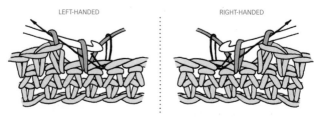

alternate decrease 2 (sc)

▶ **For half double crochet,** yarnover, insert hook in next stitch, yarnover and pull up a loop, insert hook in next stitch, yarnover and pull through all loops on hook.

LEFT-HANDED   RIGHT-HANDED

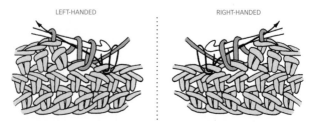

alternate decrease 2 (hdc)

▶ **For double crochet,** yarnover, insert hook in next stitch, yarnover and pull up a loop, yarnover and pull through two loops, yarnover, insert hook in next stitch, yarnover and pull up a loop; yarnover and pull through all loops on hook.

There are other variations of this decrease; the basic idea is to make the second decreased stitch slightly smaller than the first one to reduce bulk. See if you can discover your own special decrease!

LEFT-HANDED   RIGHT-HANDED

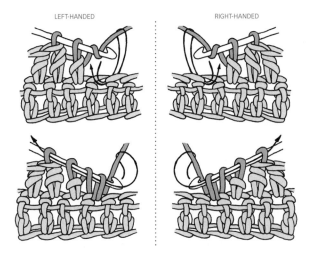

alternate decrease 2 (dc)

Q How do I make a decrease when I have to make a turning chain at the beginning of a row?

A Work the turning chain first, then work the decrease over the next two stitches in the row.

. . . .

Q How do I *increase* stitches within a row?

A Just work more than one stitch into the same stitch, giving them a common base. You can do this at the edge of a row or anywhere in the middle of a row or a round. You may also work one or more chains between stitches as an increase. The chain increase creates a hole, so it is most commonly used as a part of a larger stitch pattern. You may work these chains as stitches on the next row or round.

LEFT-HANDED · RIGHT-HANDED

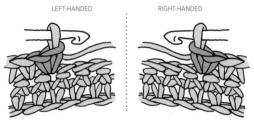

increasing in single crochet

Q What if I need to increase a large number of stitches at the beginning of a row?

A Chain the required number of stitches at the end of the previous row to act as a foundation chain, plus enough to act as a turning chain. Work the first stitch into the chain as you would on a foundation chain, then work into each chain as a stitch and continue on across the stitches from the previous row.

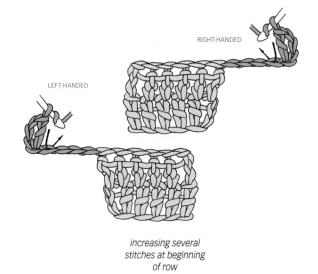

RIGHT-HANDED

LEFT-HANDED

*increasing several
stitches at beginning
of row*

Q How do I increase a large number of stitches at the end of a row?

A When you finish working the row, insert the hook into the lower left-most loop (*right-most loop for Lefties*) of the stitch just made, and work an appropriate foundation stitch. Continue working foundation stitches until you reach the desired number of additional stitches.

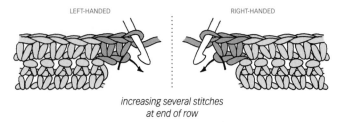

LEFT-HANDED

RIGHT-HANDED

*increasing several stitches
at end of row*

SEE ALSO: *Pages 70–84 for foundation stitches.*

Specialty Stitches

Q What is an *extended stitch*?

A Extended stitches, sometimes called Elmore stitches, are taller, slightly looser versions of the standard stitches. Each of the customary stitches can be extended to create a stitch with an intermediate height. These transitional stitches may be used to create smooth curves or a looser fabric than is possible with the standard stitch patterns. Extended single crochet is also known as *double single crochet*. Create an extended stitch by adding an extra "yarnover, pull through loop" step to a basic stitch pattern, as follows:

EXTENDED SINGLE CROCHET (ESC)

1. Insert hook into stitch, yarnover and pull up a loop; yarnover and pull through one loop on hook.

2. Yarnover and pull through two loops on hook.

extended single crochet symbol

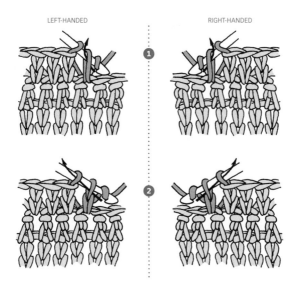

LEFT-HANDED · RIGHT-HANDED

EXTENDED DOUBLE CROCHET (EDC)

1. Yarnover, insert hook into stitch.

2. Yarnover and pull up a loop; yarnover and pull through one loop on hook.

3. Yarnover and pull through two loops on hook.

4. Repeat last step.

LEFT-HANDED

RIGHT-HANDED

extended double crochet symbol

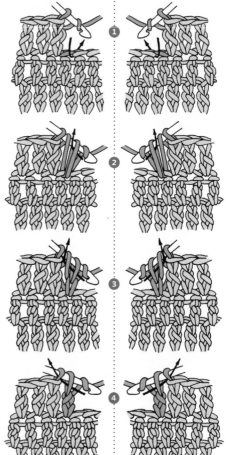

Q What is a *shell stitch*?

5-dc shell stitch symbol

A A shell, or *fan*, stitch is a group of stitches worked into the same base stitch. Crowding the base of the stitches into one spot forces the top of the stitches to spread out into a shell or fan shape. They are usually worked with an uneven number of stitches so that there is a

shell stitch

center stitch. Each stitch of a shell counts as an individual stitch, although all of the individual stitches may be referred to collectively as a shell. There are many varieties of shell stitch patterns.

Q What should I do if my shell stitch looks crowded and I can't really see the scalloped effects?

A If you are working from a published pattern, be sure you are reading the instructions carefully. Because the top of the stitches need room to spread, it is necessary to leave space on either side of the shell. Be sure to skip enough stitches between shells to show off the pattern.

Q Why is there a hole at the base of my shell?

A The many stitches going into the same base stitch cause the base stitch to become stretched, creating a little hole. If you don't like the hole, try to stretch that stitch as little as possible while making your shell stitches. If you are making up your own shell stitch design, try making shells with fewer stitches.

Q What is a *cluster*?

A A cluster is a generic term used to refer to any group of stitches that have been worked together. A cluster is made by working several partial stitches in a row, then finishing them all together

3-dc cluster symbol

with one final "yarnover, pull through all loops." The base of the cluster may be in one stitch or space, or it may range over several stitches, but when the stitch is complete and all the loops are finished off together, it counts as a single stitch on the next row or round.

One example of a 3-dc cluster might be: Yarnover, insert hook in next stitch and pull up a loop, yarnover and pull through two loops on hook; (yarnover, insert hook into same stitch and pull up a loop, yarnover and pull through two loops on hook) two times, yarnover and pull through all four loops on hook.

SEE ALSO: *Page 140 for bobbles; page 141 for puffs; page 138 for popcorn.*

Q Why is a cluster in one pattern different from other clusters in the same book?

A The term *cluster* is used to denote many different stitch pattern variations. It could refer to decreased stitches as in dc3tog; a popcorn, bobble, or puff stitch; or another variation. Always check your pattern for instructions particular to that pattern.

Q What's the difference between a popcorn, a bobble, and a puff stitch?

A Each of these related texture stitch patterns is made by working multiple increases within a small space, then decreasing within that same space. The result is a stitch pattern that pops out of the surrounding fabric. They are usually made using a variation of double crochet; the number of stitches determines the size of the popcorn, bobble, or puff. Although they are made up of multiple stitches, each is counted as a single stitch when completed. The difference among these stitch patterns is how the increases and decreases are made, and how the stitch pattern looks when complete.

Designers may use different names for the same technique, and each technique has its own variations. Be sure to check your published pattern for specific instructions for the techniques used in that pattern.

. . . .

Q **How do I make a *popcorn* stitch?**

A Popcorns can be made in double, half double, and treble crochet. Here's how:

1. Work several complete stitches into the same base stitch. When all the stitches have been worked, take the hook out of the loop. Insert the hook from front to back through the top of the first stitch of the popcorn.

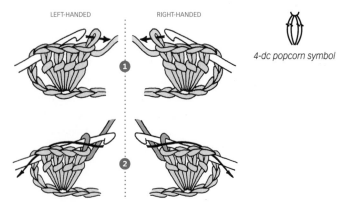

LEFT-HANDED   RIGHT-HANDED

4-dc popcorn symbol

2. Put the loop back onto the hook, and pull it through to the front to force the popcorn to "pop" off the background stitches. Another option is to yarnover after putting the dropped loop back onto the hook, and then pull the yarnover through everything on the hook.

. . . .

Q **Can I make my popcorn stitch appear on either side of the fabric?**

A Yes! When you take the hook out of the stitch, reinsert it into the stitch from front to back, and the popcorn goes to the front of the work. If you insert it from back to front, the popcorn ends up on the back of the work. You may need to use your fingers to encourage the stitches to go to the side of the fabric you want them to.

. . . .

Q **My popcorn stitch seems too loose and floppy. Can I make it look neater?**

A Here are some ways to neaten your popcorn stitch.
▶ Work the stitches on a slightly smaller hook than you have been using for the rest of the stitching.
▶ Make your popcorn stitch with fewer stitches.
▶ Make a bobble instead of a popcorn.

Q How do I make a *bobble*?

A A bobble is a specific type of cluster, made by working several stitches in the same base stitch and finishing off together. After you have worked the desired number of stitches, yarnover and pull through all the loops on the hook. Terminology varies, so always be sure to check your pattern for more specific directions.

- -

Q Can I use popcorns and bobbles interchangeably?

A Although they don't look exactly the same, you can usually substitute a bobble for a popcorn and vice versa, since both stitches, when completed, count as a single stitch. However, be consistent: Don't substitute bobbles and popcorns willy-nilly throughout your fabric.

- -

Q How do I make a *puff* stitch?

A A puff stitch is a cluster made from a series of yarnovers and pulled-up loops worked into the same stitch.

1. (Yarnover, insert hook in stitch, yarnover and pull up a loop) three times into the same stitch, yarnover and pull through all loops on hook.

2. Chain 1 to complete the puff (A) and close the top of the stitch (B).

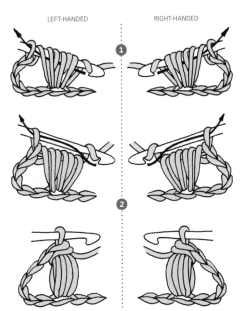

LEFT-HANDED   RIGHT-HANDED

puff stitch symbol

Q Why do my puff stitches look uneven?

A It can take a bit of practice to control the size of the loops when making a puff stitch, but it's worth the practice. Make sure that each yarnover element of your stitch is pulled up to the same diameter on your hook. Work on a swatch until you are comfortable with the consistency of your stitches.

. . . .

Q What is *bullion stitch*?

A *Bullion stitch*, also known as a *roll stitch*, is a fancy stitch made with many wraps over the hook. The size of the stitch depends on the number of yarnovers used to make it. This stitch can take some practice to master, but that shouldn't keep you from trying it. Use a crochet hook with an inline head and a straight shank, rather than one with a strong taper. Until you get the hang of it, practice with a smooth cotton, non-splitting yarn. Here's an example of how to do it:

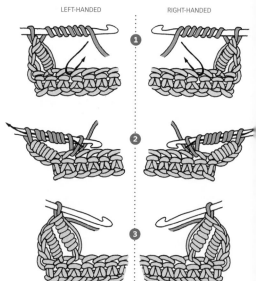

LEFT-HANDED   RIGHT-HANDED

1. Wrap yarn seven times around the hook.

2. Insert hook into next stitch.

3. Pull up a loop through the stitch *and* through all loops on the hook.

(Optional: chain 1 at end of stitch to close it.)

bullion stitch symbol

. . . .

Q Help! How do I get my hook through all those loops in bullion stitch?

A When doing the initial wraps, wrap evenly but not too tightly; you may find it helpful to place a tapestry needle or small knitting needle alongside your crochet hook to allow the wraps to be slightly larger. Now, breathe and slow down. As you reach into the next stitch to pull a new loop through everything on your hook, take your time. You may find you need to use your non-dominant hand to lift each of the loops over the hook individually or in groups of two or three. Alternatively, you may find that you can pinch the base

LEFT-HANDED   RIGHT-HANDED

using an auxiliary needle

of the loops with your non-dominant hand, and pull the hook through all the loops together in one smooth motion. If you have used an auxiliary needle to wrap the stitches, keep the needle in place and let it keep the loops open for you as you pull the hook through.

....

Q What is a V-stitch?

A A V-stitch is a combination of stitches that forms a V appearance. Although your pattern will give you specific instructions, several common ways to make a V-stitch are:

▶ Place 2 dc in the same st; on the next row work 2 dc between the stitches, rather than into them.

▶ (Dc, ch 1, dc) in one stitch or space

▶ (Dc, ch 2, dc) in one stitch or space

V-stitch symbols

....

Q How do I *link* stitches?

A Linked stitches are created from half double crochet or taller stitches. Instead of beginning the stitch with one or more yarnovers, loops are picked up from an adjacent portion of the previous stitch, thus linking each stitch to the previous stitch and making a solid fabric. Here's an example for linked treble crochet:

1. Begin with a foundation chain of the desired number of stitches, plus enough for the turning chain. Insert hook into second chain from hook and pull up a loop, (insert hook into next chain and pull up a loop) three times — four stitches are on the hook.

2. (Yarnover and pull through two loops) three times to complete the beginning linked treble.

3. Take a moment to identify the two horizontal loops on the post of the stitch you just made. Insert the hook from top to bottom under the top horizontal loop, yarnover and pull up a loop; insert the hook from top to bottom under the bottom horizontal loop, yarnover and pull up a loop; insert the hook into the next chain in the normal way, yarnover and pull up a loop. You now have four loops on the hook.

LEFT-HANDED   RIGHT-HANDED

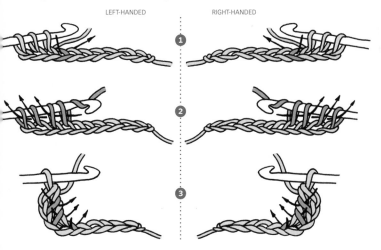

4. (Yarnover and pull through two loops) three times to complete the linked treble crochet. Continue in this manner to work across the foundation chain. For subsequent rows, work a turning chain and link the first treble to it as you did in step 1, picking up the last loop of the stitch in the top of the previous row.

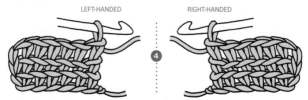

LEFT-HANDED   RIGHT-HANDED

4

Q What is a *picot*?

A A picot is a decorative element made by chaining a few stitches, typically three or four, then folding the chain in half into a tiny loop by slip stitching in the first chain or in the stitch at the base of the chain. A tighter picot can be made by working the slip stitch into the top of or into the side of the stitch at the base of the picot.

picot stitch symbol

Q What is a *crab* stitch?

A This stitch pattern is also known as *backwards single crochet* or *reverse single crochet*. It is made by working a row of single crochet in the opposite direction from the usual method: In other words, from left to right for right-handers, and from right to left for Lefties. It is often used as an edge stitch, as it creates a beautiful border.

To work a row of crab stitch, first work a row of single crochet following the normal method, so that the edge lies flat. Do not turn at the end of the row. Chain 1, then, working in the opposite direction, single crochet in the last stitch of the previous row and in each stitch across (A). Keep your crochet hook pointing left (*Lefties, right*), and use the forefinger of your dominant hand to keep the loop on the hook from popping off as you work backwards to insert your hook and pull up a loop (B). It may feel awkward at first, but after a few stitches you'll see a bumpy corded edge appear.

$\tilde{+}$

crab stitch symbol

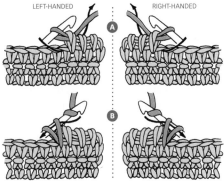

LEFT-HANDED　　RIGHT-HANDED

crab stitch

Q Is it possible to stitch into a row of backward single crochet?

A It can be done, but not very easily. Backward single crochet creates a corded edge that is usually meant to be the final row or round of a piece.

. . . .

Q How do I crochet *cables*?

A Cables are made with a combination of stitches, often front post double crochet on a background of single crochet, or treble on a base of double crochet. At even intervals a stitch is worked several stitches forward or behind the current hook position. Your instructions will indicate exactly how to make the cables.

SIMPLE CABLE

Chain 18.

ROW 1 (WS): Sc in 2nd ch from hook and in each ch across, turn.

ROW 2: Ch 1, sc in each sc across, turn.

ROW 3 AND ALL WS ROWS: Ch 1, sc in each sc across, turn.

ROW 4: Ch 1, *sc in next 3 sc, front post double crochet (FPdc) in sc in row below next sc, sc in next sc, FPdc in sc in row below next sc, sc in next 2 sc; rep from * across, sc in last sc, turn.

ROW 6: Ch 1, *sc in next 3 sc, FPdc around post of FPdc in row below, sc in next sc, FPdc around post of FPdc in row below, sc in next 2 sc; rep from * across, sc in last sc, turn.

ROW 8: Ch 1, *sc in next 3 sc, skip 2 sts, FPtr around post of next FPdc in row below, sc in 2nd skipped st, FPtr around post of first skipped st in row below, sc

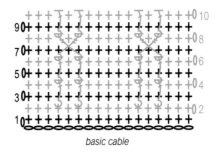

basic cable

in next 2 sc; rep from * across, sc in last sc, turn.

ROW 10: Ch 1, *sc in next 3 sc, FPdc around post of next FPtr in row below, sc in next sc, FPdc around post of next FPtr in row below, sc in next 2 sc; rep from * across, sc in last sc, turn.

Rep Rows 5–10 for pattern.

. . . .

Q What is a *selvage (or selvedge) stitch*?

A A selvage stitch is a stitch at the beginning and/or end of a row that is not considered part of the stitch pattern. Not all stitch patterns contain selvage stitches, and many that do contain them do not identify them as such. They may be plain single or double crochet stitches that serve as a stabilizing "frame" for seaming or other finishing. Sometimes any stitch at the side edge of a piece is referred to as the selvage.

More about Stitches

Q What is a *stitch dictionary*?

A This is a budding designer's best friend! A stitch dictionary contains stitch patterns that you can mix and match to make your own creations. Each stitch pattern is clearly photographed and includes information on how many multiples to chain for the foundation row. Many stitch dictionaries contain both charted and text instructions.

SEE ALSO: *Pages 247–50 for charts vs. text instruction.*

Q What is a *multiple*?

A A *multiple*, also called a stitch multiple, is the number of stitches required to work a complete stitch pattern widthwise. This set of stitches may be repeated across the width of the piece to create a pattern.

For example: A stitch pattern that uses a "multiple of 6 stitches" may be done over any multiple of 6 (including 6, 12, 18, and so on).

Some stitch patterns require a number of stitches in addition to the multiple in order to have (a) required selvedge stitch(es) or (b) to center the stitch pattern on the fabric. If a stitch pattern calls for a "multiple of 6 plus 2," it means that the stitch pattern can be worked over any multiple of 6 (6, 12,

18, 24, . . .), plus 2 stitches (8, 14, 20, and so on). Note that a multiple of 6 plus 2 is *not the same thing* as a multiple of 8, although the first multiple of 6 plus 2 is 8.

. . . .

Q What is a *pattern repeat*?

A A pattern repeat can refer to the stitches needed to complete a stitch pattern horizontally and/or the number of rows needed to complete the stitch pattern vertically. A stitch pattern that is made by working the same eight rows over and over is said to have an eight-row pattern repeat.

. . . .

Q What is the best way to learn a new stitch pattern or technique?

A Practice, practice, practice! Use a light-colored, smooth, worsted-weight yarn and an appropriate-size hook — probably an H/8 (5 mm) or I/9 (5.5 mm). In the beginning, don't worry about your gauge or about making stitches look even. Work a little swatch until you are comfortable with the stitch pattern and your edges are even. Once you are confident with the stitch pattern or technique, you can start over to work a gauge swatch or to begin your project.

SEE ALSO: *Pages 155–69 for swatching.*

If you don't understand something the first time, try approaching it through one of your other senses. Everyone has a different style of learning that works best for that person. For instance, I'm a kinesthetic learner. Reading about techniques doesn't help me unless I have yarn and hook in hand so that I can *do* as I read. You may need to look at the pictures or watch videos, because you are a visual learner. Or perhaps reading the instructions aloud helps because you learn best by hearing the words. It may help to have someone else read the instructions and explain them to you using *different* words. Videos help here, too! Whatever your learning style, do what it takes to understand a technique that is new to you.

. . . .

Q The illustrations in the book are so clear, but when I look at my work, the stitches aren't as well defined. How do I translate what I see in the book to my own work?

A It may be comforting to know that many others experience the same frustration. Realize that the illustrations must be simplified and idealized to be effective. If the illustrator drew a fuzzy strand of yarn, you wouldn't have a clue about where to put your hook! See if you can identify the main parts of the stitch, as drawn in the illustration; it doesn't matter if your yarn doesn't look exactly like the yarn pictured. You might find it helpful to have some smooth cotton yarn on hand to practice with.

CHAPTER 5

Tense about Gauge?

In the UK, gauge is known as *tension*, a term that accurately reflects many crocheters' thoughts on the subject! Gauge is nothing to be afraid of, however, and it's important, so let's take a moment to understand the concept of gauge and how to get it.

Getting Gauge

Q Exactly what is *gauge*?

A Gauge is simply a description of how many stitches and rows a particular crocheted (or knitted) fabric has within a certain area.

. . . .

Q What determines gauge?

A Gauge is dependent on a number of factors, including hook size, yarn size, your individual way of handling hook and yarn, and even your mood at a particular moment!

. . . .

Q How is gauge stated?

A Gauge may be expressed in stitches and rows per inch (or centimeter), or in stitches and rows per 4" (10 cm), with a suggested hook size. Sometimes the row gauge is omitted.

For example: 12 stitches and 15 rows = 4" (10 cm) in single crochet with J/10 (6.0 mm) hook

A gauge may also be stated in terms of number of pattern repeats or complete rounds of a motif.

For example: Two pattern repeats = 7" with H/8 (5.0 mm) hook

or

Rounds 1–3 of granny square = 3" with H/8 (5.0 mm) hook

. . . .

Q Should I always use the hook size that is given in the pattern?

A No, but it's a good starting point. It is the size the designer used to get the stated gauge with the yarn used in the project, but every individual's handling of yarns and hooks varies. Even when using identical hooks and yarns, two crocheters can get very different gauges. If you need to change hook size to obtain a stated gauge, please do so. That does not mean that you are right and the gauge statement is wrong but just illustrates the fact that gauge is achieved in a wide variety of ways.

. . . .

Q How do I figure out what my gauge is?

A You'll need to make and measure a gauge swatch: a small piece of fabric made using the same yarn, hook, and stitch pattern you plan to use for your project.

Q How big should my gauge swatch be?

A Ideally, a swatch should be no less than 4" across; 6" or more is better. The thicker the yarn, the bigger the swatch you need. The finest thread crochet swatches can be somewhat smaller. If you are working a stitch pattern with multiples, you'll need to make the swatch big enough to encompass at least one multiple.

SEE ALSO: *Page 150 for multiples.*

Q How do I make a gauge swatch?

A Start with enough chains to make an adequately sized swatch, taking care to work the chain loosely. Be sure to adjust the number of stitches to fit any stitch pattern multiples. Begin stitching, using the stitch pattern given in the gauge statement and the same hook and yarn you plan to use for the project. Different hooks, even those of the same size, handle yarn differently. Even different colors of the same yarn may work up to different gauges! Because the same yarn in different colors can yield different gauges, use all the colors in the same way you plan to use them in the finished product, if you are using more than one color.

Work in the same way the project requires (in the round or back and forth), unless otherwise stated in the pattern. Crochet at least 2", then measure to see if you are anywhere close to the desired gauge. If not, stop stitching. Start a new swatch from the beginning with a different size hook. If you are close, continue stitching until your piece is about 6" long.

. . . .

Q How do I measure stitch gauge?

A Place the swatch flat on a table. (Voice of Experience: *Do* use a flat surface, not your leg or the sofa cushion, as these surfaces aren't really flat.) Place a ruler on top of the swatch. (A ruler is preferable to a tape measure because it lies flat and doesn't stretch.) Measuring from the 1" mark, count the number of stitches to the 5" (that is 4" worth of stitches). Don't count the outer stitch or two on either edge and don't measure the first two rows or the last row, as these edge stitches are often uneven or distorted. If you don't have 4" worth of stitches, use what you have. The more stitches you can count over a longer

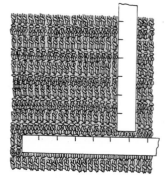

measuring a swatch

157

distance, the more accurate your results will be. Divide the number of stitches by the number of inches for your gauge per inch.

SEE ALSO: *Chapter 11, The Finish Line, for finishing techniques, washing, and blocking.*

Q What if I have a partial stitch at the 4" mark?

A Since it's hard to estimate what fraction of stitch hits right at that mark, it is more accurate to count full stitches within a certain distance. Keep counting full stitches until you reach a spot that corresponds to an easy-to-read measurement on your ruler. Make a note of what distance those stitches cover, then use that number as your divisor.

For example: If you count 19 full stitches over 4¼"

$$19 \div 4.25 = 4.47 \text{ sts per inch, or } 17.88 \text{ sts} = 4"$$

Q My stitch pattern makes it difficult to count individual stitches. How can I measure stitch gauge?

A Identify each stitch repeat in your stitch pattern. These are often a combination of stitches that are visible as a distinct unit. Count the number of pattern repeats within 4-plus inches, then multiply the number of pattern repeats by the number of stitches in each repeat and divide that by the distance over which you measured.

For example: If you count three full stitch pattern repeats over 5½", and each pattern repeat has nine stitches,

$$(3 \text{ repeats} \times 9 \text{ sts per repeat}) \div 5.5 = 4.9 \text{ sts per inch,}$$
$$\text{or } 19.64 \text{ sts} = 4"$$

SEE ALSO: *Page 150 for pattern multiples.*

The technique is the same as for row gauge, but place the ruler vertically rather than horizontally on the swatch.

. . . .

Q What should I do if my gauge doesn't match the gauge given in the instructions?

A If you did not get the gauge you wanted or expected, do not fiddle with the swatch to make it conform to your wishes, no matter how tempting! Instead, repeat the swatching process, substituting hook sizes as necessary, until you are confident that you have determined the correct hook size to give you the gauge you need.

. . . .

Q What if I have too many stitches and rows per inch?

A Switch to a larger hook to loosen up the work, which will give you fewer stitches per inch.

Q What if I have too few stitches and rows per inch?

A Switch to a smaller hook to make the stitches tighter, which will result in more stitches per inch.

. . . .

Q What if I have the right number of stitches per inch, but not the right number of rows per inch? Does row gauge really matter?

A It may not matter much, if you are close. If the pattern calls for you to work to a certain number of inches before shaping, you may be able to adjust the length of your piece without worrying about row counts.

Row gauge does matter in some cases. If you are working a piece side-to-side, especially a garment, matching row gauge can be crucial. If you are working a stitch pattern with a large row repeat as well as a stitch multiple, the placement of the rows becomes more important. For example, if the stitch pattern tells you to start shaping at row X, row gauge matters.

If you really need to match the row gauge, try going up or down in hook sizes. Sometimes this will change the row count but will not perceptibly change the stitch count. If that doesn't work, try switching brands or types of hook, using the same size that you used to get the correct stitch gauge. Make sure that you are wrapping the yarn over the hook correctly: from back to front. If the stitch pattern allows, you might be able to adjust the row gauge by working a row of extended stitches (edc vs. dc, for example) every row or every other row.

You may also be able to adjust your row gauge by making the loop you pull up through the stitch slightly longer or shorter than you normally would. However, you will have to pay attention and remember to do this consistently throughout the entire piece in order to maintain a constant row gauge.

SEE ALSO: *Pages 132–34 for extended stitches; page 71 for wrapping the yarn over hook.*

Gauge Matters

Q **What should I do with my swatch after it's finished?**

A Stop and write down what hook you used. Be specific: for example, "aluminum Susan Bates H/8 (5 mm)." Also note the name and color of the yarn, how many stitches and rows your swatch has, and what the stitch pattern is (or where it can be found in a book).

If you're close to having your desired gauge, block your swatch as you will your finished project, then measure again to make sure the gauge hasn't changed.

SEE ALSO: *Pages 298–306 for blocking.*

Q Why should I block my swatch?

A Sometimes washing and blocking changes the gauge. Unless you never plan to launder your finished item, you'll need to know how these processes affect the fabric. The yarn may fuzz up or fall apart in the wash! If it's a multicolored item, you also need to know if the colors will run. And it's best to know all this before you spend hours on stitching!

Q Why should I take measurements before and after blocking my swatch?

A The "after blocking" gauge is the one that matters the most, because that is what the finished gauge will be. Imagine how you would feel if you stitched a whole sweater and found out the gauge changed after you washed it! Be sure to note the gauge before blocking, and label it before washing it. This is the gauge that you'll have while you are stitching the fabric. Next, block your swatch and make note of the finished gauge. It is this finished gauge that needs to match the gauge stated in your pattern, unless the pattern instructions say otherwise.

Q Do I rip out my swatch now that I have gotten the right gauge?

A I wouldn't, at least not immediately. If you are running short of yarn at the end of your project, you may need to rip it out, but in the meantime, keep it around for reference. You may need to recheck your gauge down the road, and it can be useful for working out design details such as edgings and buttonholes. Also, some yarns aren't readily ripped out and reused, so attempting to unravel the swatch would be pointless. When you've collected enough swatches, you may decide to make a patchwork afghan, bag, or other item.

. . . .

Q How should I measure a thick-and-thin yarn? Aren't the results likely to differ from place to place?

A If you are using a thick-and-thin yarn, or have a complex stitch pattern, measure again elsewhere on the same swatch and compare the results. If the gauges are different, take an average.

. . . .

Q Why do published patterns always remind me to "take time to check gauge"?

A Many of us treat those reminders like we do exhortations to "eat healthy and exercise often" — something that we know we should do but just don't. However, it does save time to get the correct gauge. How long does it take to do a really good gauge swatch? And how long does it take to make a sweater, put it together, try it on, find it doesn't fit, rip it out, and restitch it? Or crochet three-quarters of an afghan, only to run out of yarn? Case closed.

. . . .

Q You're kidding. I have to do all this preparation every time?

A It's not that bad! The effort you put forth on the swatch end of things is in direct proportion to the time, money, and effort you put into the finished product. Getting the correct gauge is crucial to the success of many crochet projects, but not all. Only you can determine how much work you are willing to do in the early stages.

If you are making a scrap yarn afghan out of bits and pieces and don't care how big it is, just dive right in without swatching. Similarly, if you are making a potholder or doily, don't worry about it. On the other hand, if you are making a sweater that needs to fit a real body, it is very important to match the gauge of the pattern. In that case, time spent on the swatch is time well spent.

SEE ALSO: *Page 254 for matching gauge for a sweater.*

Q If I don't care about exact measurements, are getting gauge and blocking my swatch necessary?

A Maybe. For instance, if you are working with several different colors, washing a swatch can alert you to the possibility that colors may bleed. Also, if your gauge is off you may find yourself short of yarn. Stitching at a different gauge uses up yarn at a different rate.

. . . .

Q Help! I made a bunch of swatches but didn't label them. How can I tell them apart?

A It's probably too late for this, but in the future put a paper hang tag on each swatch as you work it. Note all the information pertinent to that swatch on the tag, and you'll thank yourself for your organizational skills!

. . . .

Q What if I can't obtain the gauge that is called for in the pattern instructions?

A Sometimes, no matter what you do, you just can't match the pattern's gauge. If you've tried everything — from changing hook sizes and/or brands to checking to make sure you are following the instructions correctly — you may have to go with your gauge and make adjustments accordingly.

Q How do I adjust for a different gauge?

A If your gauge is just a little bit off from the pattern's gauge (or if you like the fabric you get with your gauge more than with the given gauge), you can adjust the stitch numbers throughout the pattern. First, figure the conversion factor by dividing your new gauge by the gauge given in the pattern. Every time the pattern gives you a number of stitches, multiply the number by the conversion factor.

For example: The pattern gauge is 16 sc = 4", with 80 stitches in the first row to make a fabric 20" wide.

Your gauge is 15 sc = 4", or 3.75 sc = 1".

(your gauge) ÷ (pattern gauge) = (conversion factor)
15 sc ÷ 16 sc = .9375 conversion factor

(pattern number) × (conversion factor) = (revised number)
80 sts × .9375 = 75 sts in the first row

Check the math:

75 sts ÷ 3.75 sc per inch = 20" wide

Another way to do it is to calculate the numbers from scratch, using the schematic or finished measurements from the pattern.

Q Why do the instructions give two gauges?

A Different stitch patterns result in different gauges. If a project has more than one stitch pattern, the directions specify gauge for each, and you should stitch gauge swatches for each.

. . . .

Q Do I have to match the gauge on the yarn band?

A No. The gauge information given on the yarn band is just a starting point to give you an idea of what weight/size/category yarn you have and what an appropriate hook size might be for that yarn. You might find you are happy with fabric you make using that gauge, or you may find you want to adjust to suit your preferences. If you are following a published pattern, it's more important to match the gauge given in the instructions than the gauge on the yarn band.

. . . .

Q The gauge on my project isn't the same as on my swatch. Why is this, and should I worry?

A Ask yourself these questions:

▶ Did you do a large enough swatch to become accustomed to the yarn and the stitch pattern? Sometimes gauge changes as we become more familiar with a stitch pattern.

▶ Are you sure you measured your swatch accurately? Did you "cheat" to get the right gauge? Did you measure over at least 4"?

▶ Did you work your gauge swatch in the same stitch pattern you are working now? With the same hook? With the same yarn, in the same color?

▶ Have you consulted your notes? If you blocked your swatch, the gauge may have changed after blocking. If your "before" gauge is the same as what you are currently working on, you can be confident that you are on target.

▶ Could the weight of the work be elongating the stitches as the piece gets heavier? Try supporting the work on your lap as you stitch.

▶ Are you under any more, or less, stress than when you made your swatch? The stitches you made while relaxing at your mountain cabin may be different from the stitches that you make at the end of a hectic workday.

. . . .

Q **Is it a problem when my gauge changes in my swatch?**

A Yes. Try to keep an even tension on the yarn while you are working. Be sure you are holding the yarn the same way throughout. Keep working until your swatch looks even; it may take a while to become accustomed to the stitch pattern and yarn. Once you are satisfied with the uniformity of your stitching, continue working until the swatch is large enough to measure over the evenly stitched portion of the fabric.

. . . .

Q **I put down my afghan for a year, and when I came back to it, my gauge had changed. What happened?**

A Life. You may be more or less relaxed than you were when you last worked on it. You may have become more confident in your technique. You may not have used the same hook. Just change to whatever hook size you need to match your new stitches to your previous work.

CHAPTER 6

Going in Circles . . . and Squares and Triangles

Crocheting back and forth in rows is not the only way to go! Many crocheted pieces are worked from the center out, in rounds rather than rows. This method produces flat motifs and larger pieces, as well as seamless three-dimensional items. The questions and answers in this chapter cover the basics of in-the-round crochet. For a more in-depth look at motif-based crochet, refer to *Beyond the Square Crochet Motifs* and *Connect the Shapes Crochet Motifs*.

Good Beginnings

Q What is a motif?

A For our purposes, a motif (pronounced moh-TEEF) is an individual unit of crochet that can be used on its own but is more often combined with others to form a fabric. A granny square is the most common crocheted motif. Making motifs is fun and portable, because they are usually quick and easy to do, and there is an endless variety of shape and color that can be used in every one. Each is its own tiny work of art.

Q How do I start a flat piece in the round?

A The technique for working a flat piece in the round is the same whether you want your finished piece to be a circle, square, triangle, or other shape:

1. Start with a tiny center circle (called a *ring*). You can make one by chaining a few stitches, then joining the chain with a slip stitch in the first chain you made.

LEFT-HANDED RIGHT-HANDED

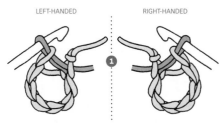

2. Work a beginning-of-the-round chain to raise the hook to the correct height for the first round, depending on what height stitch you plan to work. Work the first round into the ring.

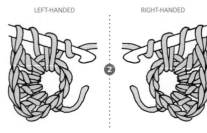

LEFT-HANDED   RIGHT-HANDED

Q Is there a trick to making the chain ring for the center?

A You'll need to chain at least three stitches to actually create the circle, but you'll probably only need to chain four to five stitches in all, just enough to get the required number of stitches into the ring on the first round, but no more. In general, a joined chain-4 ring easily holds eight stitches. A chain-5 or -6 ring holds a dozen or more stitches. This type of center ring creates a fixed-diameter center; the center ring can be quite large, if desired.

Q Is there a way to prevent the lump that occurs when I slip stitch in the first chain to form a ring?

A Instead of using the end attached to the ball when working the initial slip stitch, try using the tail end of the yarn. Or use one of the knot-less methods described on pages 173–77.

Q Are there other ways to make a starting ring?

A Another option is to work all the stitches into an extra (central) chain stitch. This makes a smaller center hole but is somewhat limited in the number of stitches it can accommodate. Two other excellent options are *adjustable ring* (or *magic ring*) and the sliding loop (or *double magic loop*). Both of these options can accommodate a large number of stitches but can also be cinched down to create an almost invisible center opening. Instructions for all three follow.

WORKING ROUND 1 INTO A CHAIN STITCH

1. Chain 2, 3, or 4 (for single crochet, half double crochet, and double crochet, respectively). In effect, this is a turning chain plus one stitch.
2. Work round 1 into the first chain you made. (You are working all the first round stitches into the extra chain.)
3. Pull tail to close center.

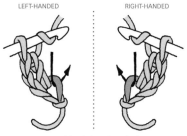

LEFT-HANDED   RIGHT-HANDED

working into extra chain

ADJUSTABLE, OR MAGIC, RING

1. Leaving a 6" tail, form a loop in the yarn and hold it in your non-dominant hand with the working yarn over your index finger.

2. Draw the working yarn through the loop so you have one loop on the hook. Chain the appropriate number of build-up chains for the first stitch.

3. Work stitches into the ring as instructed (that is, single, double, or treble crochet), working each stitch over the loop yarn and the tail yarn. When you've crocheted the last stitch, separate the tail from the loop and pull it up to close the loop.

LEFT-HANDED

RIGHT-HANDED

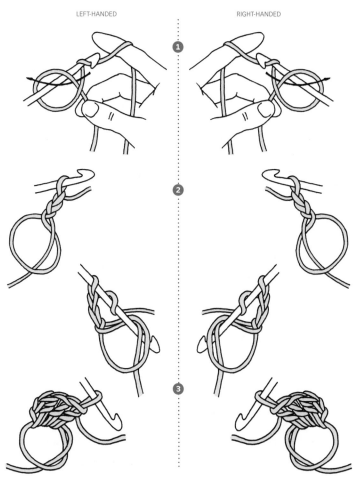

adjustable/magic ring

SLIDING, OR DOUBLE MAGIC, LOOP

1. Wrap yarn clockwise around your non-dominant index finger two times to form a ring. Holding the yarn tail between thumb and middle finger, insert the hook into the ring, grab the working end of the yarn, and pull it through the ring.

2. Chain the appropriate number of build-up chains for the first stitch. Drop the ring from the finger.

3. Working over both loops of the ring, work additional stitches into the ring to complete the first round. Before joining the first round, gently pull the beginning tail to partially cinch up the ring. You'll find that one of the ring's two strands tightens, while the other does not.

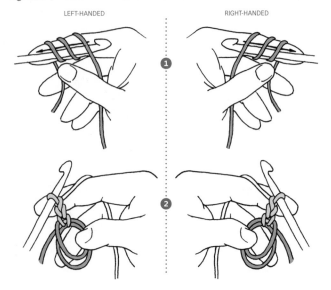

LEFT-HANDED   RIGHT-HANDED

4. Now gently tug the tightened ring until you see the other strand getting smaller.

5. When that second strand is as tight as you want it, pull the tail again to close the ring.

LEFT-HANDED   RIGHT-HANDED

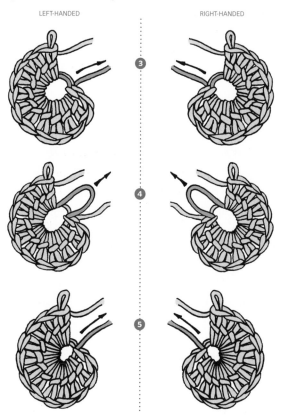

Q Can I make a larger hole in the center of the piece?

A Of course. If you are using one of the adjustable methods, just don't tighten the center hole. If you are beginning with a chain ring (and if you want a really big hole, this is what you should use) just start with a longer chain and put more stitches into the ring on the first round. Feel free to experiment with different numbers of chains in your starting ring.

. . . .

Q What does it mean to work *into the ring*?

A Instead of putting your hook into an individual stitch in your chain ring, put the hook into the center of the ring and pull up a loop around the chain. As you work the stitches, hold the yarn tail near the ring and work around it as well, to secure the tail. If you are using one of the adjustable-ring methods, insert the hook into the center of the ring and work around one or two strands of that ring.

SEE ALSO: *Pages 171–72 for starting a flat piece in the round.*

Q How many stitches go into the first round?

A That depends on both what you want your final shape to be and the height of your stitches. The taller the stitch, the more stitches need to go into the first round. Here's why: The larger a circle's diameter, the longer its circumference. The circumference of the circle is measured at the top of the stitches. Because taller stitches create a wider circle as compared to smaller stitches, more stitches are required to make a longer circumference. You'll note that the taller stitches may be crowded together at their bases but spread out at their tops to form a circle.

SEE ALSO: *Pages 186–87 for basic formulas.*

Q **How do I get in all the stitches I need in the first round?**

A Don't be afraid to squeeze the base of the stitches together. Work three or four stitches, then slide them around on your ring toward the first stitch; you should be able to snug their little feet right up next to each other. Continue to adjust the stitches as needed, but don't wait to do it until your ring is almost filled. Don't let the bases of the stitches overlap one another, or you won't be able to slide them around the ring easily. If they aren't overlapping, yet there still is not room for them all, rip out the first round and add one more chain to your beginning round, or try one of the adjustable-ring methods described on pages 173–77.

Happy Endings

Q What happens at the end of the first round?

A You have two choices: either closing the round or working in a spiral. When you close the round, you join the last stitch in the round to the first stitch with a slip stitch.

You may also keep working in a continuous spiral without closing the round. Be sure to place a marker in the first stitch of the round and move it out on each subsequent round so that you know where the beginning of the round is. You still have to work increases on each round of the spiral in order to keep the piece flat.

SEE ALSO: *Page 183 for invisible join; pages 66–68 for join with dc.*

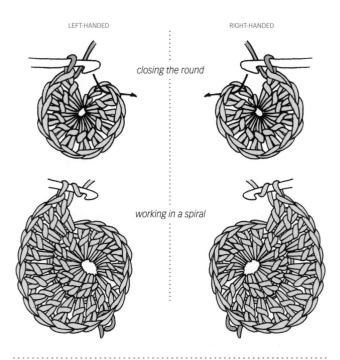

LEFT-HANDED · RIGHT-HANDED

closing the round

working in a spiral

Q What can I do to improve the slip stitch join at the end of a round?

A If you think the join is sloppy, try this alternate method of joining: Work to the end of the round, but before joining with a slip stitch, remove the hook from the loop. Insert the hook into the spot you want to join as if to make a stitch, pull up the loop you just dropped, and

181

continue. If you still don't like the way it looks, try it again, inserting the hook into the stitch from back to front and pulling through the loop.

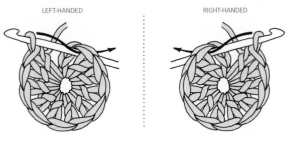

LEFT-HANDED   RIGHT-HANDED

pulling loop through back to front

. . . .

Q **Can I join a round invisibly?**

A Yes, this is a terrific way to join a round, especially the final round. Done correctly, it is impossible to see where the round ends, and if used with standing stitches at the beginning of rounds, the beginning of the round is totally obscured.

INVISIBLE (TAPESTRY NEEDLE) JOIN

1. Complete the last stitch of the round, but do not join it to the first stitch.

2. Cut the yarn, leaving at least a 4" tail, and pull up the loop on the hook until the yarn tail comes through the stitch.

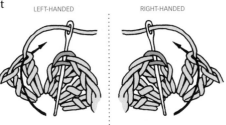

LEFT-HANDED   RIGHT-HANDED

invisible tapestry needle join

3. Thread the tail into a tapestry needle, and insert the needle under both loops of the V at the top of the first stitch of the round; pull the yarn tail through. (If you began the round with a slip knot, you'll be working over it.)

4. Insert the needle from top to bottom back down into the V at the top of the last stitch of the round.

. . . .

Q **Do I have to use both a joining stitch and a beginning chain when working rounds?**

A In crochet, you don't have to do anything! Some circularly made items, both flat and cylindrical, are worked in continuous flat spirals. When working in spiral, there's no need to use a build-up chain at the beginning of each round. Be sure to place a marker to help you identify the end of the round.

SEE ALSO: *Page 180 for working a spiral.*

Q How do I find the end of the round?

A If you are joining rounds, put a stitch marker in the top loop of the chain that begins the round. If you are working without joining rounds, slip the marker onto the first stitch of the first round. The next time around, when you work a stitch into the marked stitch, move the marker into the new stitch, and continue to move the marker on each subsequent round.

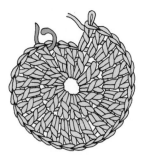

placing a marker on a joined round   *placing a marker on a spiral round*

Creating Flat Shapes

Q How do I keep my motif flat?

A Each subsequent round requires a number of increases in order to keep the piece flat, because as a circle gets larger, more stitches are needed to fill the widening circumference.

Q How do I determine how many stitches to increase each round?

A The height of the stitches determines the number of the stitches to increase on each round. The taller the stitches, the more increases you need to make.

SEE ALSO: *Page 186–87 for basic formulas.*

Q Where do I put the increases?

A The placement of the increases determines the shape of the motif. Evenly spaced increases create a circle. If you group the increases at four equidistant positions, you tend to create a square. You can make other shapes by placing increases at other points.

SEE ALSO: *Pages 171–86 for circles; pages 187, 200–203 for squares; pages 187–93 for other shapes.*

Q What kind of increase should I make?

A Any kind you want. You may work multiple stitches into the same base stitch, make one or more chain stitches, or use a combination of stitches and chains.

Q How do I make a flat circle?

A If you start with the correct number of stitches in the first round, it is fairly simple to keep up with the required increases. Increase in every stitch on round 2, every other stitch on round 3, every third stitch on round 4, and so on.

Basic Formula for a Circle

	SINGLE CROCHET	HALF DOUBLE CROCHET	DOUBLE CROCHET	TREBLE CROCHET
Chains	4	4	4	5
Stitches in ring for round 1*	6	7	11	17
Increases needed for each round	6	8	12	18
Stitches at end of round 2	12	16	24	36
Stitches at end of round 3	18	24	36	54
Stitches at end of round 4	24	32	48	72

*Not including beginning (build-up) chain of round.

NOTE: *In double and treble crochet, the beginning-of-the-round chain is counted as a stitch; in single crochet it is not. In half double crochet, there's no clear standard, but in this instance the chain is counted as a stitch.*

Q How do I make a flat square?

A Begin with a center ring as for a circle, but instead of spreading out the increases evenly, group all the increases at just four locations evenly spaced around the ring.

Basic Formula for a Square

	SINGLE CROCHET	HALF DOUBLE CROCHET	DOUBLE CROCHET	TREBLE CROCHET
Stitches in ring for round 1*	6	7	11	15
Increases needed for each round	6	8	12	16

*Not including beginning of round chain.

NOTE: *A single crochet square offers special challenges, since you must space six increases evenly at four locations. You can play with the math until it works out for your design: Put 12 increases evenly spaced every other round or increase 6 every round, alternating the corners where you put double increases.*

. . . .

Q How do I make other flat shapes?

A You can make triangles, hexagons, and other flat shapes following the same system as for a square. Begin with a center ring, and group all the increases together: in three spots for a triangle, six for a hexagon, and so on. You may need to change the number of stitches in your starting ring or your first round in order to make the stitch counts work out evenly.

SINGLE CROCHET TRIANGLE

Work through **ROUND 1** of a single crochet flat circle.

RND 2: Ch 1, *3 sc in next sc, sc in next sc; repeat from * two more times, join.

RND 3: Ch 1, sc in next sc, *3 sc in next sc, sc in next 3 sc; repeat from * one more time, 3 sc in next sc, sc in next 2 sc, join.

RND 4: Ch 1, sc in next 2 sc, *3 sc in next sc, sc in next 5 sc; repeat from * one more time, 3 sc in next sc, sc in next 3 sc, join.

RND 5: Ch 1, sc in next 3 sc, *3 sc in next sc, sc in next 7 sc; repeat from * one more time, 3 sc in next sc, sc in next 4 sc, join.

single crochet triangle symbol chart

DOUBLE CROCHET TRIANGLE

Ch 4, join with slip stitch to form ring.

RND 1: Ch 3 (counts as dc), 11 dc in ring, join. [12 dc]

RND 2: Ch 3, dc in next 2 dc, *5 dc in next dc, dc in next 3 dc; repeat from * one more time, 5 dc in next dc, join. [24 dc]

RND 3: Ch 3, dc in next 4 dc, *5 dc in next dc, dc in next 7 dc; repeat from * one more time, 5 dc in next dc, dc in next 2 dc, join.

RND 4: Ch 3, dc in next 6 dc, *5 dc in next dc, dc in next 11 dc; repeat from * one more time, 5 dc in next dc, dc in next 4 dc, join.

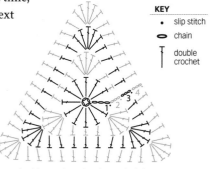

KEY

- • slip stitch
- ⊃ chain
- | double crochet

double crochet triangle symbol chart

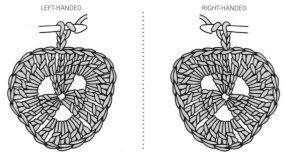

LEFT-HANDED   RIGHT-HANDED

variation on double crochet triangle

Q How do I make an oval?

A An oval or oblong shape uses elements of both back-and-forth and circular stitching. Essentially, you are making two semicircles at either end of a straight piece of crochet; the increases are grouped at the ends. The number of increases you need depends on the stitch pattern that you are working. For example, single crochet requires six increases every round to remain flat, so $6 \div 2 = 3$ increases at each end.

SINGLE CROCHET OVAL

1. Work a foundation chain for the desired length. Work 2 single crochet into the second chain from the hook. Single crochet across to the last chain.

2. Work 3 single crochet into the last chain. These increases spread out around the end of the chain. Rotate the piece so that the bottom half of the foundation chain turns to the top.

3. Keeping the right side of the work facing you, work 1 stitch into each stitch on the opposite side of the foundation chain, including the chain where you put the first 2 single crochet. You may now choose to join the round with a slip stitch. Place a marker in the last stitch. (Remember to move this marker each time you complete a round.)

4. Work the next round by increasing in each of the next 2 stitches, then work straight until you get to the 3 stitches at the other end. Work 2 single crochet in each of those 3 single crochet, then work straight to the last stitch of the round and work 2 single crochet in that stitch. (You have increased 3 stitches at each end.)

From here on out, you get to eyeball it. Keep an increase at the very end of each curve, and make the other two increases evenly spaced at increasingly wider distances from the center of the curve. It's not rocket science: As long as the oval lies flat, you're doing it right.

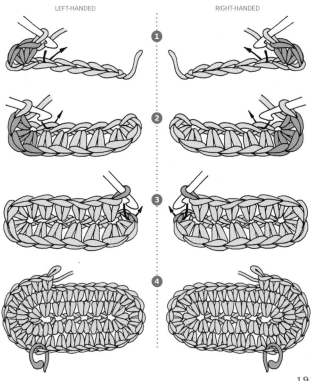

LEFT-HANDED   RIGHT-HANDED

Q I'd like to work an oval in double crochet. How many increases do I need?

A A double crochet oval requires 12 increases every round (6 increases at each end).

. . . .

Q I tried making a semicircle by working back and forth and adding half the number of increases per round needed for a circle, but the straight edge wasn't straight. Why?

A The tops of the stitches have room to spread out when you work this way, whereas in a full circle, they are crowded together and thus forced to stay in place. To solve the problem, make sure your increases are not at the edges of the semicircle, and use fewer than half the increases you would use for a circle in that stitch. For a double crocheted semicircle, crochet as follows:

CROCHETING A SEMICIRCLE

ROW 1: Beginning with one of the closed-center starts described above, ch 3 (counts as dc), 5 dc in ring, turn. [6 dc] *(This is one-half the number of stitches required for round 1 of a double crochet circle.)*

ROW 2: Ch 3, 2 dc in next dc and in each dc across, turn. [11 dc] *(This is one less increase than you make for a dc circle, resulting in fewer than half the stitches required for Round 2 of a dc circle.)*

ROW 3: Ch 3, (1 dc in next dc, 2 dc in next dc) 5 times, turn. [16 dc]

ROW 4: Ch 3, (1 dc in next 2 dc, 2 dc in next dc) 5 times, turn. [21 dc]

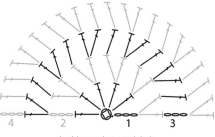

double crochet semicircle

Q Can I use more than one kind of stitch when I'm working a flat motif?

A You can certainly mix stitch heights on your motifs. Just remember to change the number of increases accordingly. For example, you start a circle using double crochet stitches, increasing 12 stitches each round. If on one round you want to use treble crochet, you must increase 18 times in that round in order to maintain a flat circle. Special stitches such as popcorns and clusters may take up a different amount of space than the standard stitches. Adjust your rate of increase to accommodate the difference.

Problem-Solving Flat Shapes

Q **I followed the instructions, but my piece isn't flat. What did I do wrong?**

A This is a common problem, and one that blocking won't entirely solve. It's better to get the structure right in the first place. Here are some things you can check:

If your crochet is curling into a bowl shape:

▶ You may not have started with enough stitches, or you may not have made enough increases per round.

▶ Add increases on one or more rounds as needed. You might be able to add a chain stitch here and there, a subtle and effective way to add stitches.

▶ Start with a smaller center ring.

▶ Even if you are increasing sufficiently, you may be working the stitches too tightly. Loosen up a bit or try a larger hook. It is even okay to change hook sizes when stitches change within the same motif, if that's what it takes to make it lie flat.

▶ Be sure you are wrapping the yarn over the hook correctly; wrapping it backward creates shorter stitches.

If the motif is ruffling:

▶ You may have too many increases per round, or too many stitches on the first round.

▶ If after counting your stitches, you find your numbers are right, you may be working the stitches too loosely. Tighten up or try a smaller hook.

▶ Start with a larger center ring.
▶ Consider making each stitch slightly taller. For example, try an extended double crochet in place of a double crochet.

SEE ALSO: *Pages 132–34 for extended crochet.*

While the charts give general guidelines for working a flat motif, you may find you have to bend the rules a bit based on your crocheting style and personal preferences. Be assured that it is okay to add or subtract increases as you work in order to have the piece lie perfectly flat. This is especially true on the longer rounds when working larger pieces.

Q Why isn't my circle exactly round?

A You may be stacking the increases on top of each other on each round. Try moving the increases so that they land at different places on each round.

Q Why does my circle look like a spiral instead of separate rounds?

A When you work the rounds, you may be failing to join the last stitch of the round to the top of the chain at the beginning of the round. Although you sometimes may want to crochet a spiral, if not, be sure that you start each round with a beginning chain in order to raise the hook to the correct height. Unless it's a single crochet, this beginning chain usually counts as a stitch. When you've reached the end of the round and made the appropriate increases, join the round with a slip stitch to the top of the beginning chain.

SEE ALSO: *Pages 87–89 for stitch heights of beginning chains.*

Q Is there another way to keep my pieces flat when I'm working in the round?

A If you prefer to be more relaxed about your stitching, you can be. Keeping in mind the guidelines above, experiment with doubling the increases every other round, or in some other arrangement. Remember that you can use a combination of chains and stitches for your increases, and that you can use a chain space in place of a stitch, as for a granny square. Just be sure to stop at the end of every round, place your piece flat on a table, look at the outside edge, and check to see that it remains flat. Be honest with yourself! Turning a blind eye won't help: If your piece is not flat on round 3, it won't correct itself on round 6.

If you notice that the last round you worked is not quite right, sometimes it's possible to make adjustments on the following round without ripping out the problem round. If you aren't happy with the adjustment round, stop! Rip out both rounds, and get it right before continuing. (Voice of Experience, from someone who abhors ripping out stitches: Sometimes it just has to be done.)

Tips and Tricks

Q **Where do I put my hook when working in rounds?**

A When you work back and forth, turning the work at the end of each row, you put your hook into loops lying sideways just slightly *to the left* of the next stitch (or for Lefties, *to the right* of the next stitch). On the other hand, when working in rounds without turning, your hook goes into loops lying sideways just slightly *to the right (left)* of the next stitch.

NOTE: *If you turn your work to the other side, you'll see this is the same spot you've been putting it in when working back and forth. The difference is that you are always seeing the right side of the fabric when you work in rounds.*

SEE ALSO: *Pages 104–11 for placing the hook and turning chains.*

LEFT-HANDED   RIGHT-HANDED

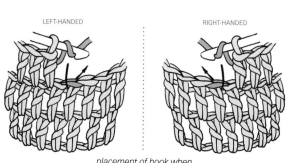

placement of hook when working in the round

Q I thought I was supposed to work in rounds without turning. Why does my pattern call this chain a "turning chain"?

A Turning chain is a generic term used to refer to the beginning-of-row or -round chain that brings your hook up to the level of the row you are about to work. Although you aren't turning your work, it serves the same purpose as a turning chain and so some patterns call it that. Other names for this are *build-up chain* or *beginning chain*.

· ·

Q My pattern says to "join with dc in top of turning chain." How do I do that?

A A typical slip stitch join brings the hook just above the first stitch of a round, ready to chain and begin the next round, but there may be times when a round ends with a chain space, and it would be really handy to have the first stitch of the next round begin just above that chain space.

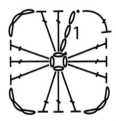

ending round with dc symbol

When the last stitch(es) before the join is a chain, you can shift the beginning of the next round by using a single crochet, half double, or double crochet as a joining stitch.

SEE ALSO: *Pages 66–68 for join with dc.*

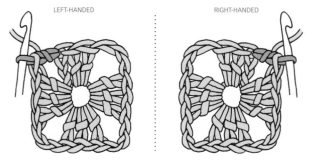

LEFT-HANDED   RIGHT-HANDED

ending round with dc

Q How can I make my motifs crisp and neat?

A There are a couple of refinements you can make for tidier motifs:

▶ Instead of starting each round in the same place, end one round and start the next one in a different spot. This prevents any build-up chains from stacking on top of one another and works especially well when you are changing colors on each round.

▶ Use standing stitches (page 67) to begin rounds and invisible joins to end them.

▶ Block judiciously (pages 298–306).

▶ Use a yarn that shows off the stitches, rather than a multicolored or highly textured yarn.

SEE ALSO: *Pages 65–68 for joining a new yarn, page 183 for invisible (tapestry needle) join.*

Q **How can I get more pronounced points at the corners of my motif?**

A Try placing a taller stitch in each corner stitch of the motif. In other words, if you are making a double crochet square, place a treble crochet in place of the center double crochet in each of the four corners. If the corner is made with a chain, make one extra chain. Try putting a picot in the corner of the final round. Experiment, as you may not need to make these adjustments on every round to get the look you want.

Granny Squares

Q **What's the difference between any old crocheted square and a granny square?**

A Although many people call any crocheted square a "granny square," the familiar granny square is a special form of square motif. Although there are many variations on the granny square, the traditional one is a double-crocheted square made with a series of chains and double-crocheted blocks.

Granny squares can be worked with any number of colors. They are a great way to use up scraps. They can be made with any size yarn and hook and can be made with any number of rounds. Make a single granny square big enough and you have an afghan!

Q How do I make a granny square?

A There are many variations on the traditional granny square. The pattern below is for a classic granny with chain-2 corners. While most instructions include a chain-3 build-up chain on every round, using standing stitches as described here makes for a much cleaner look.

TRADITIONAL GRANNY SQUARE

With A, ch 4, join with slip stitch to form ring. (See stitch diagram on next page.)

RND 1: Ch 3 (counts as dc), 2 dc in ring, *ch 2, 3 dc in ring; repeat from * two more times, ch 2, join with slip st to top of the beginning ch-3. Cut A and fasten off.

RND 2: With B, (standing dc, 2 dc, ch 2, 3 dc) in any chain space, ch 1, *(3 dc, ch 2, 3 dc) in next space, ch 1; repeat from * two more times, join with slip st to top of first dc. Cut A and fasten off.

RND 3: With A, (standing dc, 2 dc, ch 2, 3 dc) in any corner space, ch 1, *3 dc in next space, ch 1, (3 dc, ch 2, 3 dc) in next corner space, ch 1; repeat from * two more times, 3 dc in next space, ch 1, join with slip stitch to top of first dc. Break MC.

See how you are placing (3 dc, ch 2, 3 dc) in each corner ch-2 space, 1 group of 3 dc in each side ch-1 space, and 1 chain over each group of 3 dc? Once you understand that concept, you can continue making your granny square, *ad infinitum*.

SEE ALSO: *Pages 66–67 for standing stitches.*

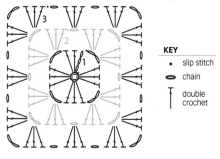

KEY

- • slip stitch
- ⬭ chain
- ⊤ double crochet

granny square symbol chart

Q Are there other kinds of squares?

A There are hundreds of variations of square motifs, as well as circles and hexagons. Entire books have been written on the subject. (For more variations on classic granny squares, hexagons, and other shapes, look for the books *Connect the Shapes Crochet Motifs* and *Beyond the Square Crochet Motifs*.) Once you are familiar with the concept of making flat motifs, you'll want to design your own.

Tubular Crochet

Q I want to work a three-dimensional shape in the round. Is it possible to crochet a tube?

A Certainly! Crochet a foundation chain with as many stitches as you need for the circumference you desire. Making sure the chain is not twisted, insert the hook into the first stitch of the chain and work a slip stitch to form a ring. Work a build-up chain (turning chain) to raise the hook to the appropriate height, then work into each stitch around. At the end of the round, join with a slip

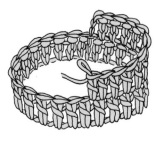

crocheting a tube

stitch to the top of the beginning chain. Repeat this round for as many times as required to get the desired length.

. . . .

Q My tube isn't straight. What makes it skew?

A This is a common problem, inherent in the stitching. It happens because the stitches are not exactly on top of each other. Because you are working in the same direction all the time, there is no opposite pull on the stitches to straighten them out. You can prevent the skewing by turning your work after joining at the end of each round.

. . . .

Q What is *amigurumi*?

A *Amigurumi* is the Japanese word for knitted or crocheted stuffed doll, but as the word is used today, it means any three-dimensional crocheted (or knitted) stuffed creature: person, animal, monster, or other imaginary persona, even food! Common amigurumi techniques include working single crochet in rounds without joining and making separate shaped pieces that are typically stuffed and sewn together. Use a smaller hook than normal to make tight stitches that will prevent the stuffing from showing through to the right side. Use purchased plastic eyes, or create facial and other features with embroidery. Creative amigurumi designers use many innovative decorative, shaping, and construction techniques in their work.

. . . .

Q **What is tapestry crochet?**

A Tapestry crochet is a multicolor crochet technique that uses tight, single crochet stitches to create a strong, sturdy fabric. It is most often used for baskets, bags, and other useful and decorative items. The color not in use is carried and caught by the working color, adding to the strength of the fabric and preventing yarn floats that could snag.

SEE ALSO: *Page 218 for working with colors.*

CHAPTER 7

A Whole Cloth

Knowing how to make individual crochet stitches is all very well and good, but good crocheters know that it's all about combining those stitches to make beautiful fabric. Now it's time now to explore the features of crocheted fabrics and the techniques used to make them.

Search for the Perfect Fabric

Q Is *fabric* really the right word to use when talking about crochet?

A Like weaving or knitting, crocheting is a method of creating a fabric. It may be lightweight or heavy, lacy or dense, smooth or textured. It may drape fluidly over the hand, or stand stiffly at attention. These fabric characteristics are a function of stitch pattern, fiber, and gauge. While there is no one perfect crocheted fabric for every use, there are features that make various ones ideal for different purposes.

. . . .

Q What is *drape*?

A The drape of a fabric is an expression of how the fabric hangs, how stiff or how supple it is. Several things influence the fabric's drape:

▶ **The gauge of the stitching in relation to the size of the yarn.** A tight gauge creates a stiff fabric.

▶ **The yarn itself.** Some yarn is naturally stiff, but it may feel less so after washing. Linen softens up considerably after washing, as do some wools. Wash and block your swatch and see how you like it then. Some less expensive synthetic yarns have a plasticlike feel that makes them more suited to craft projects than to crocheted garments.

SEE ALSO: *Pages 298–306 for blocking.*

▶ **The stitch pattern.** Single crochet fabric is stiffer than double crochet fabric. If you are having trouble getting a fabric you like with the basic stitches, try working an extended stitch to see if that loosens things up, but be aware that it may change your gauge.

SEE ALSO: *Page 132–34 for extended stitches.*

▶ **Your technique.** Relax! If your goal is a fabric with a nice, soft drape, be sure you are holding the hook gently and allowing the yarn to flow through your fingers. If the fabric is still too stiff despite your best efforts, switch to a different yarn.

. . . .

Q **Is there a right side to my fabric?**

A Probably. If you are doing a highly textured stitch like cables or bobbles, the "interesting" side is the right side. When working in rounds, the smoother side is the right side. Ultimately, however, the right side is whichever side you want it to be.

Q How do I tell which is the right side when I'm working back and forth?

A Unless your pattern says otherwise, the first row worked after the foundation chain is usually the right side. You may want to hang a stitch marker on the front of the fabric, so you'll be able to recognize the right side from the wrong side on later rows.

. . . .

Q Why are my edges uneven?

A There are several things that might be happening. You may not be keeping a consistent number of stitches on each row. Review the concept of using a turning chain as a stitch, and where to put the first and last stitches of each row. Count your stitches after every row until you are confident that you are maintaining the same number. If you are working half double crochet or taller stitches and have decided not to use the turning chain as a stitch, the turning chain itself creates a small sideways scallop every other row. If you are unhappy with the look of the turning chains, try a different method at the beginning of each row.

SEE ALSO: *Pages 105–11 for turning chains; page 107 for inserting the hook at the beginning of a row.*

Q Why is my fabric getting wider?

A There are several things that may cause this:

▶ Your foundation chain may be too tight in relation to your stitch pattern. Rip out your work and start over with a looser foundation chain.

▶ You may be increasing unintentionally. If you are using a turning chain as a stitch, you may be putting your hook into the base of the chain in every row, which creates an increase.

▶ You may have relaxed your gauge as you became comfortable with the stitching. Measure the newest part of the fabric to determine if you need to change to a smaller hook.

▶ You may have picked up the wrong hook and started using a larger hook size or a different brand of hook. Have you borrowed the hook from this project to use in a different project? Check your notes to make sure you are using the same hook you started with.

Q Why is my fabric getting narrower?

A This is a common problem. Here are possible causes, with some easy solutions:

▶ You may be decreasing unintentionally. At the end of each row, make sure you are inserting your hook into the top of the turning chain of the previous row, if the turning chain is counted as a stitch. Count your stitches after every row until you are confident that you are maintaining the correct number of stitches.

SEE ALSO: *Pages 105–11 for turning chains.*

▶ You may have tightened your gauge as you worked. Check to see if you need to change to a larger hook.

▶ You may have picked up the wrong hook and started using a smaller hook size or a different brand of hook. Check your notes to make sure you are using the same hook you started with.

Q Why is there a hole where I've been stitching?

A Here are several things to look for:

▶ You may have unintentionally skipped a stitch.

▶ If the hole is at the edge of the fabric, it could be caused by the turning chain. Try one of the methods described above to improve your edge.

SEE ALSO: *Pages 105–11 for turning chains.*

▶ If the hole occurs where you've skipped a stitch in order to decrease, use a different type of decrease.

SEE ALSO: *Pages 124–30 for decreases.*

continued on next page >>

▶ If the hole occurs where you've worked many stitches into one, as in a shell stitch, that's just a part of the stitch pattern and is hard to avoid.

▶ If the hole occurs where you started a new yarn, fix the hole when you weave in the tail.

Q Why doesn't my piece look the same when I work in rounds as when I work back and forth?

A When you work back and forth, the two different sides of stitches show on alternating rows. When working in rounds, only one side of the stitches show.

Q Is it possible to make both back-and-forth and round-and-round stitching look the same?

A Yes, it is. Here are some suggestions:

▶ **To make rounds look like back-and-forth fabric,** join the rounds at the end of each row, then turn, work a turning chain, and continue in the other direction. Doing this at the end of each round creates a fabric in which the front and the back of the stitch pattern show on alternating rounds and prevents skewed stitches.

▶ **To make back-and-forth fabric look like in-the-round fabric,** break the yarn at the end of every row and work from right to left only on each row (*left to right for*

Lefties). This is more awkward than the first method, so plan ahead. If you are making a sweater in the round, it is easier to work the rounds below the armholes as described above. You can then work the sections above the armholes back and forth, maintaining the same visual appearance to the stitch pattern.

▶ Another option is to keep the right side of the fabric facing and work alternate rows with the other hand. In other words, work one row right to left and the next row left to right. Again, it's awkward at first, but it can be done. In the process, you'll strengthen your eye-hand coordination in your non-dominant hand, and that can't be a bad thing!

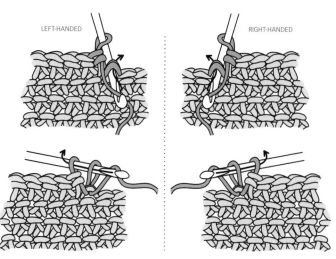

LEFT-HANDED

RIGHT-HANDED

Q Why is my rectangle skewed?

A A non-square fabric can stem from a number of sources:

▶ **Not using turning chains properly.** Be sure that all turning chains are the right height for the stitch you are using. If appropriate, treat the turning chains as stitches and work into them. If they are not treated as a stitch, do not work into them at the end of a row.

SEE ALSO: *Pages 105–11 for turning chains.*

▶ **A stitch pattern that biases the fabric.** See if you can work the stitch pattern more loosely to alleviate the bias.

▶ **A yarn that biases the fabric.** A poorly spun, unbalanced yarn may cause problems. Try a different yarn to see if the swatch is still skewed. If your pattern allows, and it is the stitch pattern or yarn that is causing the bias, you might try working back and forth in the round to see if the opposite pull of the stitches straightens the fabric.

SEE ALSO: *Page 212 for working back and forth in the round.*

Q How can I make a ribbed fabric?

A Single crochet rib is made by working rows of single crochet in the back loops only. Alternating stitches of front-post double crochet and back-post double crochet over several rows creates a ribbed-look fabric. Keep in mind that this type of ribbing does not have the same characteristic stretch as a knit ribbed fabric.

SEE ALSO: *Pages 117–118 for front- and back-post double crochet.*

Q What is *ripple stitch*?

A Ripple stitch (aka *chevron stitch*) is a type of stitch pattern that creates a sideways zigzag fabric. A series of multiple increases and multiple decreases, separated by plain stitches, forms the ups and downs of the fabric. It is a very popular stitch pattern, and there are many variations. Here's one:

CLASSIC DOUBLE CROCHET RIPPLE STITCH

SETUP: Chain a multiple of 10 + 4 (with a minimum of 24 sts).

FOUNDATION ROW: Dc in 4th ch from hook, dc in next 3 dc, (yarnover, insert hook into next ch and pull up a loop, yarnover and pull through 2 loops on hook) three times, yarnover and pull through all 4 loops on hook — *dc3tog complete*, dc in next 3 ch, *3 dc in next ch, dc in next 3 dc, dc3tog, dc in next 3 dc; rep from * to last ch, 2 dc in last ch, turn.

ROW 1: Ch 3 (counts as dc), dc in same st, dc in next 3 dc, dc3tog over next 3 dc, *dc in next 3 dc, 3 dc in next dc, dc in next 3 dc, dc3tog over next 3 dc; rep from * to last 4 sts, dc in next 3 dc, 2 dc in last st, turn.

Repeat Row 1 for desired length.

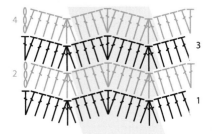

ripple stitch chart

Q I can achieve straight edges with most patterns, but I have difficulty when working ripple stitch. Is there anything I can do about this?

A You may not be working enough stitches into the beginning and ending of each row or you may not be working your edge decreases correctly. Ripple stitch rows usually begin and end with several stitches worked into the same base stitch, or with a multiple decrease. Reread your pattern instructions to see if you are following them correctly.

Q **What is felting, and how do I do it?**

A Technical answer: Felting is the process of opening up the scales of animal fibers (often using heat and moisture), interlocking them with friction, then closing them (again, often with moisture). Sounds tricky, but it's really quite easy. You've probably seen it once or twice in your life, like that time someone put your best cashmere sweater in the washer and dryer! The dense sturdy, unstretchy fabric that came out of the dryer was felt.

You can intentionally felt your crocheted fabric to make fabulous bags, rugs, and other handy items. Use a 100 percent non-superwash wool or other animal fiber such as alpaca, and stitch with a larger gauge than usual, because the stitches are going to compress and shrink when felted.

Place the crocheted item in a pillowcase and close it with a rubber band to protect your washer from excess fuzz. Place the pillowcase in the washing machine with a pair of old faded jeans or tennis balls to provide agitation. Add a little soap, and set the washer to the hottest temperature and lowest water level settings. Start the wash cycle, and allow it to run, stopping every 5 minutes or so to check the progress of the felting. As it approaches the finish line, check more frequently because sometimes the process doesn't seem to be working until it's suddenly gone too far!

When you've reached the desired degree of felting, pull out the project. Rinse it well by hand and squeeze out the excess moisture. Pull it into shape to the desired finished measurements. If it's a three-dimensional shape, stuff it with a balloon, plastic shopping bags, or other waterproof material to help it maintain its shape. Allow the piece to air dry.

Working with Color

Q How do I change colors within a row or round?

A Follow this procedure on the last stitch before you want the new color to start:

1. Work until there are two loops on the hook. Leaving a tail of about 6" of the new color, yarnover with the new color.

2. Pull through both remaining loops on hook. Now continue working in the new color.

LEFT-HANDED

RIGHT-HANDED

Q Why do my color changes look messy?

A Make sure you are starting the new color soon enough; that is, when there are still two loops of the old color left on the hook. Do this even at the end of a row/round, when the first stitch of the next row/round will be in a new color. Or for an even nicer color change at the end of a row/round, fasten off the old color and start the new color with a standing stitch.

SEE ALSO: *Pages 66–67 for standing stitches.*

If you have been securing the tail of the old color by working over it in the new color stitches, you may be getting some telltale color showing through. Wait until the piece is finished to worry about those ends, then work the tails into the back of the same-color stitches.

You could be having problems with the tension on the old and new stitches; if so, simply adjust the size of the stitches when you weave in the ends.

Q How do I incorporate two or more colors on the same row or round?

A Work with only one color per stitch. The challenge is what to do with the other color. The solution depends on how far the other yarn has to travel to its next stitch. You may carry the unused yarn loosely across the back of the work (called *stranding*), catch it behind/under the stitches you are working, or drop it and start a new length of yarn for each section of color (called *intarsia*).

. . . .

Q How do I strand colors?

A **Method 1:** When you reach the color change, simply drop the color you just used (color A), pick up the new color (color B), and work a section in color B. When you pick up color A again, be sure to leave a bit of slack in the "float" behind color B so that the fabric is not distorted. You can carry both yarns across a row or throughout a round in this manner. If the floats are more than a few stitches wide, hold the unused yarn at the top of the previous row and work around this strand every few stitches when you are working with the other yarn, or use Method 2.

Method 2: Holding the unused yarn at the base of each stitch, work the new stitches over the stranded yarn, as you do when securing yarn tails. When working in the round with right side facing at all times, hold the unused yarn slightly to the back (wrong side).

SEE ALSO: *Pages 294–297 for securing tails.*

Q How do I work *intarsia*?

A Intarsia uses separate lengths of yarn for each section of color. Start by determining how many different color sections you will be working across the row, and cut a corresponding number of yarn lengths in the appropriate color. The length of each separate yarn may vary based on the area to be stitched. Work in the first color (Color A) as indicated, then drop color A and begin the next color (Color B), allowing Color A to hang on the wrong side. When you have completed the B section, start with a new, separate length of Color A (or the next color), and continue across the row, using a separate piece of yarn for each color section. On the following row, the color or yarn you need should be waiting there for you to pick up as you come to each color change. If you prefer, you can work from full balls of yarn rather than shorter strands, but take care to rearrange the yarns as needed to prevent them from tangling.

Remember to start each new color on the last "yarnover, pull through" step of the old color to avoid color bleed.

Q How do I decide which method to use?

A Sometimes this decision is a matter of personal preference. Stranding usually works well for two or three colors that alternate across a row. Hiding the unused yarn behind each of the contrasting-color stitches allows you to switch back and forth easily between the two colors. However, because it creates a thicker fabric than intarsia, it is usually unsuitable for more than two colors at a time. It may also be difficult to hide a highly contrasting color within the stitches.

When you have large blocks of color, or units of color that are isolated, intarsia is usually the most appropriate method. Use intarsia when the length between colors makes it difficult to do stranding or when the number of colors used in a row would make stranding impractical.

As always, it's a good idea to practice your color technique on a swatch before beginning your project.

. . . .

Q **My yarn gets tangled on the wrong side when I work with colors. Am I doing something wrong?**

A You aren't doing anything wrong; it's just a feature of some types of color work. Some crocheters wind lengths of yarn onto yarn bobbins to make the yarns more manageable. Others prefer to cut long lengths of yarn and allow them to hang out and look messy on the wrong side of the work, pulling each strand free of its brothers as they work (my favorite). Still others prefer to use one of several types of commercially made yarn holders.

If you alternate the way you turn the work at the end of each row (clockwise one time, counterclockwise the next) the colors will untwist themselves every other row. This only works, however, if you don't twist the colors when you pick up a new color; just drop the old color and hold it to the right *(Lefties: to the left)* when you pick up the new color.

. . . .

Q Why does my fabric pucker when I'm working with different colors?

A You are pulling the yarn floats too tightly across the back of the fabric. Take care to allow plenty of slack as the unused yarn travels across the back of the stitches. You may want to use one of the other color methods instead.

. . . .

Q Can I carry unused yarns up the side of the fabric?

A If the yarn doesn't have to travel very far (no more than a few rows), it's fine to carry an unused yarn up the side of a piece. Make sure you keep it loose, and catch it once or twice in a turning chain. However, cut the yarn and start it again if you are using lots of different colors. If carried vertically, several yarns together create too much seam bulk.

. . . .

Q I was carrying my yarn up the side, but now it's on the wrong edge when I need it. What happened?

A When there are an even number of rows between color changes, you drop the old color (A) and begin working with the new color (B), working forward across the row, turning and then working back to the original location, so you come right back to where you dropped A. If, however, you work an odd number of rows in each color, the dropped yarn gets stranded on the wrong edge when you need it in order to begin the next row. To work around this problem, depending on the stitch pattern, it may be possible to omit the turn on certain rows by moving your hook to where the other color is and working another right- or wrong-side row with it.

For example, for one-row stripes worked back and forth:

ROW 1 (RS): Work in A; turn.

ROW 2 (WS): Work in B; do not turn.

ROW 3 (WS): Move back to color A and work with it, then turn.

ROW 4 (RS): Work in B; do not turn.

Repeat Rows 1–4.

. . . .

Q **I'd like to try a pattern with a picture. Can you advise me on how to manage the colors?**

A Graphs indicate where to put the colors. When it's time to change colors, use the same method as for adding a new yarn: Work until the last two loops are remaining on the last stitch of the old color, then yarnover and finish the stitch with the new color and continue working.

SEE ALSO: *Page 220 for stranding; pages 221–22 for intarsia.*

Q How do I read a color graph?

A Each square in a color graph indicates one stitch as it appears from the right side of the fabric. Each horizontal row of squares of the graph indicates a row or round of stitching. Starting at the lower right-hand corner of the graph (*Lefties: lower left-hand corner*), read each square from right to left (*Lefties: left to right*) for a right-side row. Turn the work, then read each square on the second row from left to right (*Lefties: right to left*).

If you are working in rounds, read every line from right to left (*Lefties: left to right*), since the right side of the fabric faces you at all times. If you are working back and forth in rounds to look like back-and-forth stitching, treat it as you do row-by-row stitching.

A graph often has heavy vertical lines indicating a pattern repeat. Work the area between these lines as many times as necessary across the width of the piece, or as directed.

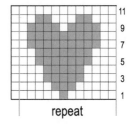

repeat

CHAPTER 8

Pattern Language and Symbols

While many crocheters happily stitch along, making up their own projects without ever following a published pattern, others like to follow a pattern. For this, you need to be able to understand written pattern instructions. Some patterns are written with text only, some written mostly with symbols, while others are a mix of the two. You'll find handy lists of common crochet terms and symbols in the appendix, pages 369–96.

The Anatomy of Patterns

Q Published patterns seem to be written in a different language! How do you go about "translating" them?

A If you're put off by written instructions because they look complicated, think of them as a recipe. Most people are comfortable with reading recipes because they are familiar with cooking terminology and abbreviations. If you take the time to become comfortable with crochet jargon, you'll be well on your way to following any written pattern. Read this chapter, and refer to pages 369–96 for more on standard crochet abbreviations and common crochet phraseology.

· ·

Q What do well-written patterns have in common?

A Although crochet patterns may not be standardized, well-written patterns have a lot in common. Before you start a pattern (even better, before you buy!) look for the following features:

▶ Information on yarn weight and content

▶ Gauge, usually over at least 4" in the main stitch pattern, and sometimes in all stitch patterns used in the project

▶ Suggested hook size to achieve gauge

▶ A list of abbreviations using standard abbreviations whenever possible. Any special abbreviations or techniques are clearly explained.

▶ Often, a combination of text and symbols for stitch patterns, allowing you to choose the format that works best for you

▶ A stitch key for symbol diagrams

▶ A range of sizes. The best garment patterns have complete information on sizes, sleeve lengths, neck width, and so on. Much of this information may be shown on a schematic drawing. The more information you have, the easier it is to make a garment fit well.

SEE ALSO: *Page 231–32 for schematic drawings.*

▶ Easy-to-read print.

▶ If applicable, information on stitch pattern multiples. This data simplifies pattern adjustments.

SEE ALSO: *Page 150 for stitch pattern multiples.*

If these attributes are missing, it can be a red flag that the pattern might be lacking crucial information and might be hard to follow. The best instructions have not only been written to certain standards, they have been checked by editors and perhaps by test stitchers for accuracy. This won't eliminate all errors, but it sure does help make it easier to follow the instructions. If you think your pattern is not up to snuff, simply find another one. There are plenty out there to choose from!

Q I've never followed a pattern before. Where do I begin?

A Start by looking at the preliminary section that describes materials needed, gauge, and size information. Take a look at the schematic drawing, if one is given. If it's a garment written in multiple sizes, choose your desired size. Choose a suitable yarn, then scan the how-to-stitch section for an idea of how the project is constructed. You may not understand everything at the first reading, but you'll get an overview of the pattern and notice if anything in particular jumps out at you. It's usually easier to follow the pattern once you have yarn and hook in hand.

Q How do I know if a pattern is too difficult for me?

A Some pattern publishers designate skill levels as beginner, easy, intermediate, and advanced to suggest the ease with which certain types of crocheters may be able to follow a pattern. These labels can be somewhat arbitrary, however, as many of us have some mix of beginner and more advanced skills. Some pattern will designate "skills used" in a design, which may be somewhat more helpful. However, if the instructions are well written, even beginners can learn advanced skills. Let skill designations be a guide, but not a rule, when choosing patterns.

Q **If skill levels aren't given, how do I know if I can follow the pattern?**

A Scan the pattern to see if you recognize the stitches and techniques used. Ask yourself these questions:

▶ Is the pattern well written?

▶ Do I understand the techniques used?

▶ If I'm not familiar with the techniques used, am I willing to learn them?

▶ Does it have shaping? If so, just a little or a lot?

▶ Is it an easy-to-see stitch pattern worked in an easy-to-see-yarn? Does that matter to me?

Don't let anybody tell you that you can't stitch something. If you are willing to learn new techniques, you can do it!

Q **What should I expect to see under "materials"?**

A This is the ingredients list of your crochet recipe, the items that you need to gather in order to make your project. It's a good idea to collect all of them before you begin stitching, although you may want to wait to purchase buttons until you can try them with your finished fabric. The materials list may include the following:

▶ Recommended yarn, including company name and name of yarn, yarn weight, size of balls/skeins, amounts in yards/meters, and fiber content

▶ Suggested size and type of hook(s). Remember: This is just a suggestion. Use the size you need to get the gauge called for in the pattern. If a hook other than a standard style hook is needed, the pattern will say so.

▶ Stitch markers, a tapestry needle, and any other tools you may need to complete the project. (Voice of Experience: Sometimes the pattern omits these items, especially scissors. You *always* need scissors.)

▶ Plastic rings, buttons, and any other trim items needed for the project.

Q **Why do I need to look at the gauge statement before I even get my yarn?**

A If you have been crocheting for a while, you know that the suggested gauge can give you an idea of the size/weight of the yarn called for in the pattern. It also gives you an idea of how heavy the fabric will be and, if you are using a yarn other than the yarn called for in the pattern, what kind of yarn you should use. In some cases, you may find (to your delight) that gauge is not crucial in the project.

Q **What is a schematic, and why is it important to review it?**

A A schematic is a graphic representation that includes the dimensions of the pieces of a project. It is often shown at the end of a pattern, but it is important to look at it before you start stitching because it contains a lot of useful information.

A schematic shows the shape and proportion of each stitched piece, so you can have an idea of what shape you are creating. It may show details such as pocket placement and neck or edge treatments. If the garment is made in one piece, the schematic indicates that.

If the shaping of the front and back are similar, often only the front schematic is given. If the sweater is a cardigan, you may have only one half of the front. Don't worry, there's still plenty of information given! You can look at a schematic and determine where you might need to make size adjustments: longer or shorter sleeves, wider neckline, and so on.

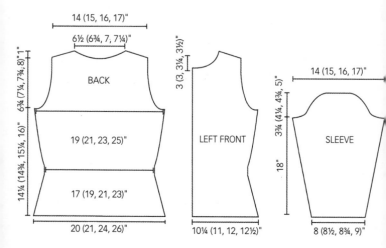

Size Matters

Q **Why are some sizes written within parentheses?**

A When instructions for more than one size are given in the pattern, the numbers within the parentheses indicate the number corresponding to a particular size. You may find it easier to follow the instructions if you circle the numbers for your size with a pencil or highlight it with marker throughout. Here is a typical example:

Sizes: Small (Medium, Large, Extra Large)
Finished Chest Sizes: 38 (42, 46, 50)"

In the above example, the number for the smallest size is first, followed by the number for each subsequent size in that same order within the parentheses. In this case, size Small has a finished chest measurement of 38"; size Large has a finished chest measurement of 46".

Sometimes both parentheses and brackets are used to denote several sets of measurements:

Sizes: Child's S (M, L, XL) [Adult's S (M, L, XL)]

SEE ALSO: *Pages 257–61 for more on sizes and fit; pages 257–258 for ease in sweaters.*

Q Can I just assume that size Medium will fit me, just as it usually does?

A Just because you wear a size 7 shoe, you wouldn't buy any size 7 shoe without trying it on! Don't assume you wear a size Medium because you always wear a size Medium. The medium size may just be the middle size given in the pattern. You'll have to determine what the designer means by "medium."

. . . .

Q So how do I know which size to make?

A Use all the information that the pattern instructions give you to determine what size is best for you. Look at the information about finished measurements that you find at the beginning of the instructions and in the schematic. Compare the finished measurements with a garment that fits you well and is of similar style and weight. Choose the size that results in the closest match to your desired finished chest/bust measurement. Remember, you can always shorten or lengthen the sleeves and bodies of garments.

If you don't have a finished garment to measure, look at the finished measurements and compare them to your actual body measurements. Take into account how much ease you will need to get the silhouette you want for that garment.

SEE ALSO: *Pages 257–61 for more on ease and measurements.*

Q What's the best way to take body measurements?

A For hats, measure around the fullest part of the head, keeping the tape level and snug around the forehead. For socks, place a ruler on the floor next to your foot; measure from the back of the heel to the tip of the longest toe. Also measure around the widest part, usually around the ball of the foot. You may also choose to measure sock height from the floor (heel turn) to the length desired.

SEE ALSO: *Pages 257–61 for measuring and sizing for sweaters.*

Pattern Talk

Q What does "increase every sixth row" mean?

A Work five rows even, then increase on the sixth row. Increases are on rows 6, 12, 18, 24, and so on. Alternatively, you can increase on the first row, then work five rows even, placing increases on rows 1, 7, 13, 19, and so on.

Q Why are there *Pattern Notes* or special instructions?

A Some pattern directions highlight information that is important for you to know before beginning. Be sure to read these carefully. Some examples you may run across include, "Yarn is used double throughout" and "Body of sweater is worked in one piece to underarm."

. . . .

Q What does *continue in this manner* or *continue as established* mean?

A Say you've been increasing, decreasing, or working a particular stitch pattern. When you come to these instructions, you simply keep doing what you've been doing, following whatever the immediately preceding instructions say to do.

. . . .

Q Why is stitch pattern listed?

A If a stitch pattern other than single, double, or treble crochet is used, it is often written out in full before the instructions for the piece. The stitch pattern multiple should also be given. The instructions usually tell you to work your gauge swatch in this stitch pattern.

SEE ALSO: *Pages 155–57 for gauge swatch.*

Q Do I have to memorize all of those abbreviations and symbols?

A Don't worry! Both text- and symbol-based instructions usually include a key explaining every abbreviation, symbol, or special stitch used in a project. Any unusual symbol is also accompanied by a text explanation of how to execute the stitch. If it's not listed on the pages right next to the project, look in the front or back of the book, magazine, or pattern.

While there are some more-or-less standard abbreviations, standardization is relatively new to the crochet world. It's a good idea to check the abbreviations every time you start a new project. In time, you'll find you've memorized the most common abbreviations without even trying.

SEE ALSO: *Pages 369–72 for abbreviations.*

Q All these punctuation marks are giving me a headache. Why are there so many?

A Your high-school English teacher was right: punctuation matters. In our written language, punctuation marks show us where to pause and collect our thoughts before continuing on through a paragraph. In crochet patterns, they serve the same role by helping us move through a row. Each pattern publisher has its own punctuation style, but there are many similarities from pattern to pattern.

▶ **Periods** usually mean the end of a row.

▶ **Semicolons** are often used mid-row to set off a series of instructions.

▶ **Parentheses** may be used to denote sizes, as described earlier in this chapter.

▶ **Parentheses** are also used to set off stitches to be worked as a group. These sets are followed by a number indicating how many times to repeat the group.

> *For example*: (Yo, pull through 2 loops on hook) 3 times.
> *Translation*: Yarnover, pull through 2 loops on hook, yarnover, pull through 2 loops on hook, yarnover, pull through 2 loops on hook.

▶ **Parentheses** also may indicate steps to be done all into the same stitch.

> *For example*: (sc, hdc, dc, hdc, sc) into ch-3 space.
> *Translation*: Into the next space made by 3 chains, put a single crochet, half double crochet, double crochet, half double crochet, and single crochet, in that order.

▶ **Brackets or braces** may be used instead of, or in combination with, parentheses to set off more complicated instructions.

> *For example*: [(dc in next dc, ch 1, skip 1 dc) two times, dc in next dc] two times
> *Translation*: Into the previous row of double crochet stitches, work double crochet, chain 1, skip 1 double crochet, double crochet, chain 1, skip 1 double crochet stitch, double crochet (that's the first whole set written with brackets), double crochet, chain 1, skip 1 double

crochet, double crochet, chain 1, skip 1 double crochet, double crochet.

▶ **Asterisks** indicate a point of repeat.

For example: Ch 1, sc in same stitch, *ch 1, skip 1 stitch, sc in next stitch; repeat from * two more times.

Translation: Chain 1, single crochet in same stitch, chain 1, skip 1 stitch, single crochet in next stitch, chain 1, skip 1 stitch, single crochet in next stitch, chain 1, skip 1 stitch, single crochet in next stitch.

Some directions are worded "repeat from * twice," instead of "repeat from * two more times." Both examples mean the same thing: specifically, that you should work through the entire set of instructions from the asterisk (*) to "repeat from" once, then repeat that section two more times, for a total of three times.

▶ **Repeat from * across row** means to work the instructions after the asterisk as many times as needed in order to reach the end of the row. If you don't finish your row at exactly the end of the repeat, you've done something wrong.

Exception: Repeat from * to last 3 stitches, end sc in last 3 stitches.

Translation: You are to repeat the pattern until there are only 3 stitches left in the row, then work 1 single crochet into each of the next 3 stitches to end the row. If you don't finish the repeated portion of the pattern with 3 stitches left to go on your row, you've done something wrong.

▶ **Daggers (†) and double asterisks (**)** are sometimes used in combination with other punctuation to designate repeated sets. Other times they denote an incomplete pattern repeat, offering a stopping point for the last repeat of the row or round.

For example: Ch 1, sc in first sc, *ch 2, sc in next sc**, ch 2, dc in next sc; rep from * around, ending last rep at **

Translation: The last stitch of the round will be a single crochet.

....

Q **What if different punctuation marks are used in the same row?**

A This means that there are multiple steps within a row. You still follow a prescribed order for the steps. Start at the beginning of the row or round, and do each step as it comes. When you reach a set of parentheses or brackets, follow the sequences as described above as many times as necessary, then move on to the next step. For example, here's what you might find for a border written for working around an afghan:

Ch 1, *[sc in next 2 sts, (sc, ch 5, sc) in next st, sc in next 7 sts] to corner st, (sc, ch 5, sc) in corner st, sc in next 5 sts; rep from * around.

Translation:
▶ ch 1 to begin the round;

▶ *sc in each of the next 2 sts, (sc, ch 5, sc) in the next st, sc in each of the next 7 sts;

▶ repeat the line above until you reach the corner stitch;

▶ work (sc, ch 5, sc) in the corner stitch;

▶ sc in each of the next 5 sts;

▶ repeat the entire section from * along each side of the afghan until you reach the beginning.

....

Q I get confused when pattern instructions use asterisks and say to "repeat x times" while others say to do something within the parentheses a certain number of times. How many times do I work the instructions after the asterisks or between the parentheses?

A Let's use this example:

"Do this, do that; rep from * three times."

vs.

(Do this, do that) three times.

Think of it this way: you can't repeat something until you have done it once, so any time the instructions say "repeat from *", you work the instructions after the * once, then work them again the number of times indicated.

In the first example above, you "do this, do that" a total of four times: once, then repeated three (more) times.

In the second example, you "do this, do that" a total of three times.

However, a warning is in order here: there are some designers who do not understand this concept, and who do not follow this convention. If the pattern is not working out, try working the instructions a different number of times to see what works — or contact the publisher or designer for clarification.

. . . .

Q **I thought I did what the instructions said, so why don't I come out with the right number of stitches at the end of the row?**

A Double-check your work to make sure you understood and followed the instructions correctly. Did you treat the turning chain properly, counting it as a stitch (or not), according to the instructions? Sometimes you can fudge a stitch or two to make it come out right, even if you did make a mistake. However, if you are going to be able to see the mistake, or if it will have undesirable consequences on future rows, you'll have to rip out the row and start again. If you just can't get it to work, perhaps there is a problem with the pattern.

SEE ALSO: *Pages 105–11 for turning chain; page 244 for finding pattern help.*

Q Why are there extra numbers at the end of a row? I don't have enough stitches to work them.

A You may be confused by the stitch count at the end of a row. When the stitch count has changed during a row because of increases or decreases, most patterns give you an updated stitch count so you can check your number.

For example: You start with 21 stitches on a row. The next row says: Ch 3 (counts as dc), dc in same st, dc in next 19 sts, 2 dc in turning chain. [23 dc] You have increased one stitch at the beginning and at the end of the row, resulting in 23 double crochets.

Be aware that this stitch count number may be punctuated in a number of different ways. It may be in parentheses or brackets (as shown), or it may simply stand alone between periods or after a dash.

Q I've tried and tried — why can't I get the pattern instructions to come out right?

A Of course, your pattern instructions may have a mistake! Here are some ways you can check yourself *and* the instructions.

▶ Try drawing each row/round out in symbols to see if it works.

▶ Try having someone read the pattern to you while you stitch, or try saying it aloud to yourself as you stitch.

▶ Ask for help from a more experienced crocheter.

▶ See if you can find an errata sheet for the pattern, either online or through the publisher.

▶ Above all, use your common sense. If you can see what the pattern is supposed to do, just go ahead and do it.

SEE ALSO: *Page 390, To Learn More*

Q Where can I find pattern help?

A That depends on the pattern. If you need help with basic crochet stitches and techniques, study this book or other books, or use online resources. If the pattern instructions themselves are the problem, check out the website of the pattern publisher. Both large publishers and independent designers often have errata pages on their websites, where they post any known pattern errors and the fix to them. You may also check Ravelry and other social media sites to find comments made by other crocheters who have made the same pattern. As a last resort, you may contact the publisher (or designer) directly if you think you have found an error that has not shown up on your online search.

SEE ALSO: *Pages 390–96 for resources; page 391 for Ravelry.*

Q I'm left-handed, and the instructions aren't working for me. What should I do?

A Most crochet instructions are written for right-handed crocheters, those who work from right to left across a row. Often it doesn't matter which way you work, but sometimes if you stitch from left to right across a row, the instructions don't work for you. Try substituting "left" for "right" and "right" for "left" in the instructions you are reading.

SEE ALSO: *Pages 23–24 for more on left-handed crocheting.*

Q What does *RS facing* mean?

A RS is the right side of the fabric, the side you want to show to the public. When the instructions note the right side is facing you, it means that you are holding the piece with the right side toward you and you are about to stitch across it.

Q What does it mean to "end with a wrong-side (WS) row"?

A Ending with a wrong-side row means that the last row you work is a wrong-side row. Finish stitching a wrong-side row, then move on to the next step in the instructions. If the instructions say to turn at the end of the wrong-side row, you'll be continuing on a right-side row.

Q How do I keep track of my place in patterns?

A Try one or more of the following techniques:

▶ Make a photocopy of your pattern, and put a pencil mark on the copy as you finish each row (or each step). Please make photocopies for your own use only, not for sharing with your friends (see page 251).

▶ Enlarge the pattern on a copier to make it easier to read.

▶ Use a magnet board and stand, moving the magnet up as you work each row.

▶ Use a sticky note or highlighter tape to mark your place.

▶ Keep a notepad handy, and jot down where you stopped.

▶ Load the instructions onto your electronic device as a PDF document, then use a reading application that allows you to highlight or mark your place within the document.

▶ Buy a supply of hang tags, and put them on your work each time you leave off, with a note reminding you where you left off. (Thanks, Maggie Righetti!)

▶ For complex stitch patterns or garment instructions, write each row on a separate index card. Punch a hole in the corner of each card, and tie them together in order. Work Row 1 from the first card, flip it out of the way, work Row 2 from the next card, and so on.

▶ Practice "reading" your actual work so that you begin to see what needs to be done next. As you become comfortable with a stitch pattern, you'll develop the ability to work without referring to the written instructions.

. . . .

Q Why do some patterns have stitch symbol diagrams?

A In many countries, and increasingly in the United States, crochet instructions rely on symbols instead of, or in addition to, text to indicate placement of stitches. Each type of stitch is represented by a symbol that resembles that stitch. The stitches that have been introduced in this book have included the most common symbol for each stitch, to help you become familiar with them. If you are learning to crochet, it's just as easy to learn the symbol (and the abbreviation) at the same time you learn the stitch.

. . . .

Q Why should I bother to read and become familiar with symbol crochet?

A Because the symbols resemble the stitches they represent, symbol crochet allows you to see what the stitch pattern is supposed to look like and to see the relationship of stitches to one another. You can see exactly where to place each stitch and what shape the final stitches take. You can see at a glance the type of stitches used. Many crocheters find this way of presenting patterns easier to follow than written instructions. Having a visual aid can help you avoid mistakes before they happen.

Another advantage to learning this system is that you can read patterns from any country. For example, you'll find that stitchers in Japan are doing amazing things with crochet.

. . . .

Q **How do I understand the symbols?**

A Consult the chart key on pages 88–89 and on pages 369–73 to become familiar with each symbol. You'll note that there is a certain logic to the symbols: a row of chain stitches looks like a chain, a double crochet is taller than a single crochet, and a treble crochet is taller still. The tall stitches each have hash marks on them to distinguish their height (and if you think about it, the number of hash marks on dc and tr indicate the number of times you "yarnover, pull through 2 loops" to get the loops off the hook). Front post and back post symbols have little "hooks" at their base, which reminds you that *your* hook goes around a post. Front loop only and back loop only symbols look like the front loop and back loop of a V, and appear between the stitch the hook goes into and the base of the stitch you are creating.

Symbols may be stretched, skewed or bent in order to re-create the shape they take in the actual fabric, but the basic form of the symbol remains the same. The bottom of the symbol indicates which space or stitch your hook goes into, and the upper portion of the symbol tells you which type of stitch to make. For example, the 3-dc cluster on page 136 shows 3 double crochets worked into the same base, and finished off all together as 1 stitch.

The symbols presented in this book are just one version of symbols you might see in modern American patterns. Different publishers have different styles; sometimes the hash mark on a stitch is tilted and sometimes it is straight. Sometimes a single crochet is shown as **+** and sometimes it is shown as **✕**. Different countries may use different symbols entirely. Don't panic if you see a symbol you don't know — there should always be a stitch key somewhere nearby! You may even discover that you can interpret new symbols without a lot of trouble, once you understand the basic symbols and their variations.

··

Q **How do I read a symbol crochet diagram?**

A First make sure you understand the different stitches that are used in the diagram. Rows are numbered alternately on the left and right edges of the chart, indicating in which direction right-handers will work each row. Rounds are numbered along the right edge only. Alternate rows/rounds are sometimes in different colors to help you differentiate between the rows. There may be a section of repeated stitches, which indicate that you work that set of stitches a certain number of times as needed.

Begin with the required number of foundation chains (count them on the chart) or a center ring, and continue "reading the picture" as you make each stitch, placing the hook and making the stitch as indicated.

Sometimes symbol diagrams show just a portion of the stitch pattern, indicating the beginning and end of a row or round, and some, but not all, of the stitches in between. However, this type of diagram will start you off with enough information to show what is going on in the "missing" part of the diagram.

For practice reading a stitch diagram, accompanied by text instructions, look at the examples on pages 188, 193, 202, and 338.

. . . .

Q How do I read a symbol chart if I'm left-handed?

A Symbol charts are written for those who stitch right-to-left. You'll have to remember to start each row on the opposite side of the chart and read in the direction that you are stitching. You may find it helpful to scan the stitch chart and flip it vertically to make it easier to read. For motif-style charts, simply read the stitches in a clockwise direction.

Q What's the difference between "dc in next 2 dc" and "2 dc in next dc"?

A In the first example, you are putting a double crochet stitch into the top of each of the next two double crochet stitches, as in "dc in each of the next 2 dc." In the second instance, you are putting two double crochets into a single base: the top of a double crochet.

· ·

Q What is the difference between "sc 1" and "1 sc"?

A Probably nothing. Different pattern publishers have different writing styles.

Finding and Using Patterns

Q How does copyright apply to me?

A All written crochet patterns and articles are copyrighted, whether or not they say so explicitly. As such, they should not be photocopied or shared electronically without permission of the copyright holder. It is neither ethical nor legal to copy a pattern to give to your best friend, even if the pattern is no longer in print. It is neither ethical nor legal to make copies of instructions from a book so you can teach from it. And in many cases, it is neither ethical nor legal to buy a pattern and then crochet many copies of the item to sell at a craft fair.

If you want to obtain permission to share a pattern, write to the publisher, who will put you in touch with the copyright holder. This may be the author or designer of the published pattern, or it may be the publisher.

There is one exception to the restrictions on copyrighted material: if you bought the pattern and would like to make a copy for yourself so that you can see it better, carry it conveniently in your crochet bag, or make notes on it without altering the original, no special permission is required.

. . . .

Q Where can I get free patterns?

A Yarn companies often give away patterns with a yarn purchase, and most have free patterns available on their websites. In fact, there are thousands of free patterns available on the Internet. Do a search for "crochet patterns," or look at To Learn More, page 390, to get a start on finding free patterns.

Remember that patterns from individuals on the Internet may not have been edited for clarity and accuracy. If you are a beginning crocheter, you should probably start by using an edited pattern from a well-known yarn company site or from a reputable self-published designer.

SEE ALSO: *Page 244 for pattern help.*

CHAPTER 9

No-Sweat Sweaters

Some people crochet for years and never make a garment. If you don't want to make your own great-looking, perfectly fitting sweaters, that's fine, but don't let Sweater Fear keep you from trying. Making a sweater or other fitted garment is an opportunity to synthesize gauge, stitch patterning, reading patterns, fit — and perhaps even design — all in one project. Answers to your questions are below, so pick a great pattern and get started!

Analyzing the Swatch

Q I'm making a sweater for the first time. Do I need to match the gauge exactly?

A Yes! As I mentioned in chapter 5, if you are making a sweater that needs to fit a real body, it is very important to match the gauge of the pattern. Let's look at an example:

Gauge in instructions: 4 sc per 1"

Desired finished bust measurement: 42"

You therefore need 4 sts × 42" = 168 stitches for the circumference of the sweater. If you are even just a half stitch off per inch, it can make a huge difference. Here are some examples:

▶ If your gauge is 3½ sc per inch and you follow the pattern instructions as written, your finished sweater will be 168 sts ÷ 3½ = 48" around, or 6" too large!

▶ If you work the same sweater with a gauge of 4½ sc per inch, the finished sweater will be 168 sts ÷ 4½ = 37" around, or 5" too small!

....

Q How do I estimate the yardage for a sweater, based on my swatch?

A Basic information for swatch calculations (by weight or without a scale) can be found on pages 51–54. Essentially, you'll need to calculate the yarn amounts used in the swatch, then apply that to the finished measurements of your intended project. But for a sweater, the calculation is a bit more complicated. Here's the formula to estimate the amount of area in a sweater with a front, back and two sleeves:

(Total finished chest measurement × Length of sweater)
+ [(Width of top of sleeve + Width of sleeve cuff)
× Length of sleeve] = Total area of sweater

With this information, you can estimate what you'll need for your finished project by making the following calculation:

[Area of project × Number of yards (meters) in swatch]
÷ Area of swatch = Number of yards (meters) needed for project

Divide the yards (meters) by the number in each ball, then round up to the next whole number to get the number of balls needed. OR

[Area of sweater × Weight of swatch] ÷ Area of swatch
= Weight of sweater

Divide the weight of the sweater by the weight of one ball, then round up to the nearest whole number to get the number of balls needed.

And remember, this is just an estimate! It's always safer to buy an extra ball. When you finish a project, make a note of how much yarn you used so you can refer to it in the future.

Getting Oriented

Q How do I approach a sweater pattern?

A Just as you might glance at a map before leaving on a long trip, it's a good idea to do a quick read-through of the pattern to orient yourself as to what to expect when you are making a garment. Check that you have the proper materials and that the pattern has the expected information. Determine ahead of time if the sweater is made all in one piece or made in pieces and seamed together. Is it worked bottom-up or top-down? Are there any terms you are unfamiliar with, and are they explained in the pattern? Once you have an idea of where you are going, the journey will be much smoother.

SEE ALSO: *Pages 227–28 for well-written patterns.*

Q Are subheadings important?

A Knowing where you are and what you are about to do is very helpful when making any project! In a sweater pattern, each portion of the garment is labeled: Front, Back, Sleeves. You may also see subheadings where shaping takes place, such as "Neck Shaping." Hat patterns may have headings for Brim and Crown.

Q How do I tell the Left Front from the Right Front of my sweater?

A Sweater pieces are described as they are worn, so the "Right Front" of a sweater is the piece for the front right side of your body. "Back Left Shoulder" is the part of the sweater Back that will be on your left shoulder when you wear the sweater. It's okay to hold pieces up to your body to figure this out!

. . . .

Q What is the difference between *Back* and *back*?

A Many patterns capitalize the parts of the sweater, so "Back" is a piece of a sweater. Lowercase *back*, on the other hand, usually refers to the work as you hold it: The "back" of the stitch is the side away from you or the "back" could be the wrong side of the fabric.

Making the Right Size

Q Why are body measurements and finished measurements different in the pattern?

A The difference between the wearer's body measurements and the finished sweater measurement is called *ease*. Ease is necessary for a good fit, but it varies according to the style of the sweater and the weight of the yarn. It may also take into account the wearer's preference for how the garment will fit.

Body-hugging sweaters have little ease, while more casual sweaters and coats have a great deal of ease. The outside measurement of a sweater made with bulky yarns may differ from its measurements inside, next to the body. Since measurements are taken on the outside of the garment, bulky sweaters must have more ease to result in the same fit as a sweater made with thinner yarn.

SEE ALSO: *Size Matters, page 233.*

Q **What's the best way to take body measurements for a sweater?**

A Measure over your normal undergarments. Measure over the fullest part of your chest/bust, making sure the tape measure is parallel to the floor. Hold the tape so that it is not slack, but don't pull too tightly, either.

Also measure from the bones at the center back of your neck to your wrist with your arm extended horizontally ("Center Back to Cuff" measurement), and across

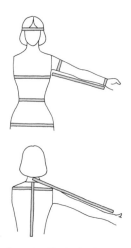

silhouette of body showing points of measurement

your shoulders from the tip of one shoulder to the tip of the
other shoulder ("Cross-Back" measurement). Depending on
the garment, you may want to know your upper arm measurement at the widest point, and/or your hip or wrist measurements. For length, measure from the bone at the center back
of your neck to your waist or to your desired sweater length.

**Q How do I measure a curve when figuring armhole
height?**

A You probably don't have to measure the curve. Even
curved armholes and necklines are measured on a
straight vertical line from the beginning of the shaping to
the top.

Q What if I need to make a sweater shorter or longer?

A Unless you are working a complicated stitch pattern in
which the row count matters, simply start any armhole
shaping sooner (or later) than the pattern suggests. If the
stitch pattern is complex, you should probably start the shaping on a repeat of the same row of the pattern as designated.
Start neck shaping when the height of the armhole is the
same length as that given in the pattern. It is important to
keep the distance between the beginning of the armhole
shaping and the top of the sweater the same length as the

original, because that measurement corresponds to the top-of-sleeve measurement. If you change the length of the armhole, you must also adjust the sleeve cap shaping. When adding length to a sweater, remember that you'll need more yarn than the pattern calls for.

. . . .

Q What if I need to change the sleeve length?

A Changing sleeve length is a bit more complicated than changing body length, because sleeves are usually shaped from the cuff up to the shoulder. A change in sleeve length without changing the beginning and ending widths requires a change in the intervals between the shaping rows. A longer sleeve has more widely spaced increase rows; increase rows on a shorter sleeve are closer together.

Decide how long your sleeve needs to be. If it is less than an inch shorter than the given sleeve length, you may simply put a couple of the increase rows a bit closer together than the pattern suggests. If you need to make your sleeve just an inch longer, you may modify the pattern and crochet a couple of more rows between two of the increase rows. However, if you need to change the sleeve length by more than about 1 inch, some math is in order:

Desired length of sleeve to widest point	−	Length of cuff or lower edge	=	Length available for shaping
Length available for shaping	×	Row gauge	=	Number of rows available for shaping
Number of stitches needed to increase	÷	2	=	Number of times to increase on each side
Number of rows available for increase	÷	Number of times to increase on each side	=	How often to increase (in rows)

"How often to increase" will probably not be a whole number. Just round it to the nearest whole number and increase that many times, or work increases on rows alternating between the two nearest whole numbers.

Getting in Shape

Q **How do I accomplish "reverse shaping"?**

A Some shaping, such as for armholes or neck curves, takes place on one edge of the fabric. The instruction "reverse shaping" means that you have worked one piece of a

reverse shaping

garment and now need to work a mirror image of that piece. You accomplish this by working the same directions for the second piece, but doing the shaping on the opposite edge of the fabric. For example, with right side facing, on a cardigan's Right Front, the armhole shaping is done on the left edge of the fabric and the neck shaping takes place on the right edge. The Left Front armhole shaping takes place on the right edge of the fabric and the neck shaping on the left.

To understand how the shaping works, you may find it helpful to draw out the shaping using symbol crochet, so you have a diagram of what's happening on both sides of the garment.

SAMPLE SHAPING FOR A DOUBLE CROCHET CARDIGAN

For example, a typical pattern may read as follows:

RIGHT FRONT: Work until piece measures 14" from beginning, ending with a WS row.

ARMHOLE SHAPING

RS: Ch 3 (counts as dc), dc to last 7 dc, turn, leaving remaining stitches unworked. (This produces a decrease of 7 sts)

WS: Ch 1, slip stitch in same stitch and in next 2 dc, ch 3, dc in each stitch to end, turn. (This produces a decrease of 2 sts) Work even until armhole measures 5½" from beginning of shaping.

LEFT FRONT: Work as for Right Front, reversing shaping.

Here's how to follow the above instructions:

▶ On the Right Front, you work the first armhole shaping row by stopping short of working a full row. For the Left Front, work the same number of rows until you reach the armhole shaping. (Voice of Experience: Don't just measure. Count the rows.)

▶ Now you are about to work a right-side row and need to shape the armhole at the beginning of the row, not at the end as you did for the Right Front. Here's how: Slip stitch across the first 7 stitches to move the hook and yarn across to the spot where you need to begin the row. (Remember: Slip stitches do not add height to a row.) You may also want to slip stitch into the next (eighth) stitch to put the yarn exactly under your chain. Now ch 3 to start the row, and work all the way to the end.

▶ Next row (WS): Ch 3, work across the row until 2 stitches remain, turn, leaving remaining sts unworked. Work even until armhole measures 5½".

Q **Can I avoid stair-step shaping on the neck and armholes of a piece?**

A Many published patterns give shaping instructions that leave a stair-step edge at the neck and armholes. It can be difficult to work with these jagged edges; a smooth curved edge is much easier to seam or finish with a border.

To refine the shaping of a curved edge, take advantage of what you know about stitch heights: decrease the height of the last stitch or two of a shaped edge. For example, on shoulder shaping your pattern might read: "Ch 3, dc to last 3 sts. Fasten off." This creates a shorter row by omitting the last 3 stitches, but leaves an abrupt angle where the double crochet ends. Instead, you could work, "Ch 3, dc to last 5 sts, hdc in next st, sc in next st. Fasten off." This creates a more gradual slope.

gradual shaping

SEE ALSO: *Page 87 for stitch heights.*

Putting It All Together

Q How do I assemble my sweater pieces?

A Sweaters worked in pieces are usually put together in the following order.

1. Join shoulder seams.
2. Work front and neck borders, and possibly lower edges.
3. Set in sleeves.
4. Sew body and underarm seams.
5. Work lower edge if not already done.

For comfort, use a seaming method that creates little bulk on the inside of the sweater. Experiment to determine the best method for your sweater. You may slip stitch or whipstitch the shoulder seams from the wrong side. You'll probably want to use mattress stitch to work the side and underarm seams, as it makes a flexible, virtually invisible join. Some people prefer to use slip stitch or single crochet to join all sweater pieces.

....

Q How do I insert a zipper into a sweater?

A First, choose a zipper appropriate for your garment. Heavy-weight separating zippers are suitable for outer garments like heavy jackets and coats. Medium-weight zippers are meant for cardigans. The length of the zipper should match the length of the opening. Here's how to do it:

INSERTING A ZIPPER

1. Sew as much of the sweater together as possible, leaving the zipper for last.
2. With the right side facing, pin one edge of the zipper to the wrong side of the fabric, taking care to keep it in a straight line with the fabric's edge. *To hide the zipper,* make the edges of the crocheted fabric cover the center of the zipper. *To feature the zipper as a design element,* place the center of the zipper a bit farther away from the fabric's edge.

continued on next page >>

3. Baste the zipper in place with sewing thread.

4. Repeat this process on the other side of the zipper, centering the zipper between the fabrics. Check to ensure that the basted-in zipper is straight.

5. On the right side, with sewing thread in the same color as your yarn, back stitch the zipper in place near the edge of the fabric.

6. On the wrong side, whipstitch the outer edges of the zipper to the fabric.

. . . .

Q **What stitch pattern is best for a zipper placket?**

A The edge of the crocheted fabric should be finished with a firm, straight border, such as two or three rows of single crochet. A final row of reverse single crochet makes a nice decorative edge.

SEE ALSO: *Chapter 10 for borders, buttons, and buttonhole bands; Chapter 11 for finishing techniques.*

On the Edge

A crocheted border can provide a stabilizing or decorative finished edge to a crocheted fabric. Many knitted sweaters have crocheted borders, and there are even entire books dedicated to crocheted edgings. You'll find the basics here, but see Books (page 395) for some additional suggestions.

Crocheting Borders

Q Where should I put my hook when picking up stitches along an edge?

A Always work the first row of an edging with the right side facing you.

▶ **If you are picking up along an upper horizontal edge** and the stitch gauge is the same for the border stitch pattern as for the main piece, you'll probably work into both loops on every stitch of the last row.

▶ **If you are working on the opposite edge of the foundation chain,** you are holding the piece upside down and stitching into the unworked loop of the foundation chain.

▶ **If you are picking up along a side edge,** you have to judge how far into the edge and at what intervals to put a stitch, based on the fabric and the size of the stitches

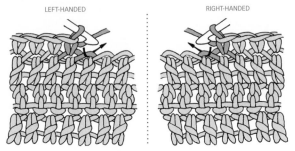

LEFT-HANDED   RIGHT-HANDED

*working on the opposite edge
of the foundation chain*

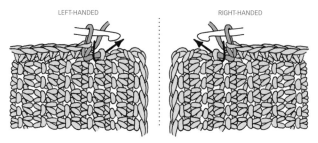

LEFT-HANDED   RIGHT-HANDED

picking up along a side edge

you are making. Insert the hook into a stitch, rather than into the space between stitches. If you work into the space, you create unsightly holes along the edge. If you are working a single crochet border on the side of a single-crocheted fabric, put a stitch in about every row of the edge. If you are working a single crochet border along the side of a double-crocheted fabric, you may need two stitches in every row.

Q **What if the gauge of my border stitch pattern is not the same as the gauge of my fabric?**

A You may have to make adjustments. On a horizontal edge, using your swatch as a guide, experiment to see if you should stitch into 3 out of 4 stitches (for instance, 1 stitch in each of the next 3 stitches, skip 1 stitch), into 5 for every 4 (for instance, 1 stitch in next 3 stitches, 2 stitches into next stitch), or some other combination. Do the same thing along a vertical edge, calculating how many stitches you need to put into each row along the edge. Your goal is to crochet a border that lies flat, without drawing in or flaring out. The most important thing is consistency. Take care to insert the hook the same distance into the fabric throughout the edge, and space the stitches evenly.

. . . .

Q **How do I "pick up stitches" evenly along an edge?**

A If you followed my earlier advice about making a swatch, you can use your swatch to help you. Using a ruler, place markers at 2" intervals along the edge of your swatch. If the border will be worked on both horizontal and vertical edges, be sure to mark both. Using the same number of stitches between each mark, stitch the border you'd like to use on your larger piece. If you're working from written instructions, there will be instructions for the border, possibly including the number of stitches to use. If you're adding a different border pattern, or if the specific instructions are not given, or if you cannot achieve the same gauge stated in the instructions, you may have to experiment to get the border to lie perfectly flat. When you are happy with the results, make a note of how many stitches you have within each 2" space on your swatch.

SEE ALSO: *Pages 155–69 for gauge swatch.*

Now mark 2" intervals on your larger piece, and work the same number of stitches between the marks as you worked on your swatch. It's usually easy to keep track of the number of stitches within that short distance. (Voice of Experience: Of course, you may skip practicing on the swatch, but you'll have more to rip out if you don't get it right the first time.)

. . . .

Q Why doesn't my border lie flat?

A It sometimes takes several tries to get this right. Start by analyzing what's happening; then you know what approach to take to correct it:

▶ If the border is ruffling, you may have too many stitches. Rip it out and start over with fewer stitches. You can also try a smaller hook, but be careful not to work the edging too tightly.

▶ If the border is pulling in (*cupping*) you may need to rip it out, then add more stitches or use a larger hook.

Sometimes a border looks fine on the first few rows or rounds but starts to misbehave as you work farther. If this happens, use the same logic for adding or subtracting stitches described on pages 272–73 to make it lie flat.

Q Can I stitch a continuous border around a piece without turning?

A Yes. Pick up and work stitches along each vertical and horizontal edge as described above, but when you reach a corner or a curve, make certain adjustments to allow the edging to lie flat. (See the next question.)

Q How do I make my corners lie flat?

A For outside corners, think about turning a corner in a car: The outside wheels have to travel farther than the inside wheels to make the turn. The same principle applies when you work an edging on a crocheted piece. The outside rows/rounds have to travel farther than the inside rows/rounds, so you have to add stitches to increase the distance along the outer edge at each corner.

For example, on the first row/round of a single crochet border, work 3 single crochet stitches into each corner stitch. When you

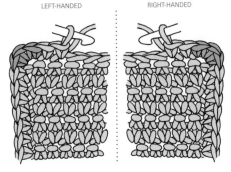

LEFT-HANDED   RIGHT-HANDED

increasing in the corners

finish these 3 stitches, mark the center stitch of the 3-sc group, then when you come to that center stitch the next time around, work 3 single crochet stitches into it.

If you are working double crochet, put 5 stitches into the corner stitch on every row or round. In some cases on the final row/round of a border, you can put fewer increases at each corner to soften the edge.

For inside corners, the rows/rounds must get shorter rather than longer. Here you will have to *decrease* at the corners, usually working a double decrease for single crochet (3 sts to 1), or a quadruple decrease for double crochet (5 sts to 1).

. . . .

Q **Why won't my neck edge lie flat?**

A Make sure you are happy with the look of the first round/row of edging you worked. Does it lie flat? Are there the same number of stitches on each side of the neck? Are both sides of the front neck symmetrical? If so, on the next rounds/rows, you may need to do the opposite of what you do on outside corners. A neckline is a circle that gets smaller as the width of the neck border increases. Each subsequent round/row of the border needs to be a bit smaller than the previous ones. Putting a few decreases on each row/round usually solves the problem. The best place to put these decreases is usually in the front and back "corners" of the neck and at each shoulder.

Q I tried to pick up stitches evenly along my edge, but the first row still looks sloppy. How can I fix it?

A It can be difficult to make the first row or round of an edging look good, especially if it is in a contrasting color. You are making decisions about where to put each stitch, and if you have to skip a stitch here and there along the main fabric, the result can be an uneven-looking edge. Try working the first row/round with the same color as the main fabric, then stitch subsequent rows/rounds with the contrasting color. Be sure you have measured and are picking up stitches evenly and consistently throughout.

SEE ALSO: *Page 270 for horizontal and vertical pick-up on edges.*

Q How do I make a *picot edge*?

A A picot edge is a nice touch for a simple edging, and it's very easy to make.

Begin by working a row/round or two of single crochet along the edge. If working in rounds, join with a slip stitch.

Work the picots on the final row/

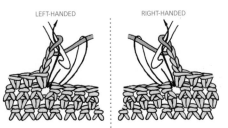

LEFT-HANDED   RIGHT-HANDED

round as follows: Chain 1, *sc in next sc, ch 3, sl st in same st, sc in next 2 sc; rep from * to end of row/round. Join with a slip stitch if working in rounds, and fasten off.

. . . .

Q How do I make a *shell edge*?

A This classic edge is a great choice for any crocheted piece. Begin with a single crochet base row in a multiple of 6 stitches plus 1. If you are working in the round, begin with a multiple of 6.

▶ **To work the final row:** Chain 1, sc in first stitch, *skip 2 stitches, 5 dc in next stitch, skip 2 stitches, sc in next stitch; repeat from * across. Fasten off.

▶ **To work the final round:** Chain 1, sc in first stitch, *skip 2 stitches, 5 dc in next stitch, skip 2 stitches**, sc in next stitch; repeat from * around, ending last repeat at **, join with slip st to first sc. Fasten off.

Q **What if I don't have the right multiple of stitches for the final edging row/round?**

A You can work an additional row/round of single crochet, increasing or decreasing a few times as needed to give you the desired multiple. Or just adjust the edging a bit, adding or subtracting a stitch between the pattern elements to make it come out right. As long as it looks good to you, it's right.

Q **What are some other edging options?**

A Your options are limited only by your imagination — and by the number of stitches available to you. There are thousands of stitch patterns that could be used as borders, and with a bit of ingenuity (and keeping in mind stitch multiples and what you know about getting corners to lie flat), those stitch patterns can be engineered to go around corners without breaking the design. See Books (pages 395–96) for some additional suggestions.

Buttons and Buttonholes

Q Which comes first, the buttons or the buttonholes?

A If possible, choose the buttons first, then make the buttonholes to custom-fit the buttons.

. . . .

Q Do you have any advice about choosing buttons?

A Choose a button in keeping with the style of the garment. Bulky outerwear usually requires large buttons, while lightweight lacy cardigans call for dainty buttons. If you are designing your own garment or want to make changes to a published pattern, before beginning the garment, decide whether you want the buttons and button bands to be a part of the design of the sweater or to be unobtrusive. Calculate the number of buttons you need by deciding how much space you want between buttons. Modesty may require more buttonholes on a garment meant to be worn next to the skin and which has little ease built into the design, while outerwear, which normally has more ease and is worn over other clothing, may require fewer buttons. If your sweaters often gap across the bust, an extra button or careful placement of buttons can prevent that dreaded "gaposis."

SEE ALSO: *Pages 257–58 for ease.*

Q How big should my buttonhole be?

A A buttonhole should be only as big as it needs to be in order to get over the button. Buttonholes that are too big look sloppy and don't hold. Loop-style buttonholes often stretch, so they may need to be a bit smaller in the beginning.

. . . .

Q Which comes first, the button band or the button-hole band?

A When working bands onto completed pieces, make the button band first. When the buttonholes will be integral to the main piece, make the button side first. You can use the button side to help determine buttonhole placement.

. . . .

Q Where do I put buttonholes?

A Current fashion dictates that buttonholes go on the right front for women and on the left front for men. (I always have to go to the closet to check my other garments when it's Buttonhole Time, or remember that "women are right.")

Even if you are following a pattern that gives instructions for buttonhole spacing, it's a good idea to double-check their placement before working the buttonholes. This is especially true if you have added or subtracted length from the sweater, as you'll also have to adjust the buttonhole spacing.

Top and bottom buttonholes are usually ½" to 1" from the beginning of neck shaping and from the lower edge. If you are adding a neck border after the button border, take into consideration the width of the neck border; you may need to place the top buttonhole in the neck border and space the others evenly between. Most published patterns include this information.

Of course, buttons don't have to match in an evenly spaced, tidy line down the front of your sweater. You can use a single button at the neck, or put groups of 2 or 3 down the front. Use your imagination.

. . . .

Q **How do I space buttonholes evenly?**

A Start by determining the placement of your top and bottom buttonholes. If you are adding the buttonhole band, mark the side that will hold it. If you are working buttonholes as you work the piece, mark the opposite side and add buttons to correspond to the markers as you crochet. Mark these places with a stitch marker, coiless safety pin, or piece of thread. You now have a couple of options for figuring the spacing for the remaining buttonhole placement:

OPTION #1: THE MATH-WHIZ WAY

1. With the crocheted piece flat on a table, measure the distance between the markers at the top and bottom of the garment.

2. Divide this distance by the number of remaining buttonholes, plus one. That is, if you need four more buttonholes, divide by 5.

3. Using a ruler, place markers at the intervals you determined in Step 2.

OPTION #2: NO MATH REQUIRED

This method works if you have an odd number of buttonholes. I always try to have an odd number of buttonholes so I can use this method!

1. Fold piece in half so that the top and bottom buttonhole markers are together. Place a third marker at this fold, and unfold the garment.

2. Fold again so that center marker and top marker are together. Place a fourth marker at this fold, and unfold.

3. Fold again so that center marker and bottom marker are together. Place a fifth marker at this fold, and unfold.

4. If necessary, continue to split the difference between the markers until the desired number of holes is marked.

marking buttonholes by folding

Q **How do I make a *chain-and-skip buttonhole*?**

A This is a most popular buttonhole. It works well for single and half double crochet bands but may be too loose for double crochet or taller stitches. It's easy to adjust the size of the buttonhole for different size buttons: Just skip additional stitches and work additional chains. Start with a base row of single crochet.

CHAIN-AND-SKIP BUTTONHOLE

1. Place markers at each spot where you want a buttonhole. Single crochet to the marker, *chain 1 (or more), skip 1 stitch (or more; skip the same number of stitches as you made in your chain), single crochet to next marker; repeat from * until all buttonholes are complete, then work to end of row/round.

2. On the next row/round, put one single crochet into the chain space for each stitch skipped.

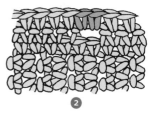

1 **2**

Q Are there other buttonhole techniques?

A Of course! Here are two more to try.

▶ A **simple chain loop** is easy to execute and can be sized to fit any button. It is worked on the final row of a band, but it may stretch out or be too flimsy for some fabrics. To make a chain loop buttonhole, follow step 1 under chain-and-skip buttonhole above, then work to the buttonhole mark, chain the minimum number of stitches required to reach around the button, stretching it slightly, then stitch in same stitch or in the next stitch, and continue working the band to the next mark.

simple chain loop buttonhole

▶ **A covered chain loop** is stronger and looks more finished than a simple chain loop. Here's how to do it:

1. Make the covered chain loop on the last row of the band by working past the buttonhole marker, then chaining the number of stitches needed to go around the button. Remove the hook from the chain, and insert it into the border several stitches back, then into the last chain made; pull the chain through the border stitch so that the loop is centered over the marker.

2. Single crochet into this chain loop as many times as necessary to cover it, then continue with the border until the next buttonhole marker. Practice this on a swatch, and try it with your button before working it on your finished garment.

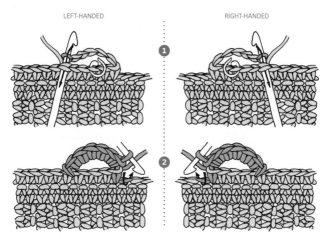

LEFT-HANDED   RIGHT-HANDED

covered chain loop buttonhole

Q How do I know which buttonhole method to use?

A Remember that swatch? When you are checking the button band or edging pattern on the edge of the swatch, go ahead and practice some buttonholes at the same time. You can try making different-sized buttonholes on it until you get one that looks pleasing, is stable, and exactly fits your button. If possible, it's best to buy your buttons before making the buttonholes. Then you can choose the method that works best for your garment/button combination.

. . . .

Q I have rather large buttons and I'm having trouble aligning the buttonholes. Any tips?

A Keep in mind that the marker indicates the center of the buttonhole. If you are using a chain-and-skip buttonhole, start a stitch or two before the marker. You may want to try a loop-style buttonhole that extends out from the edge of the fabric.

Another alternative is to use backward-buttoning buttonholes for large buttons. Sew the large button on the front of the band, with a smaller button on the wrong side of the band, creating a button shank between the

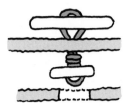

two buttons. Make buttonholes to fit the smaller buttons, and button them backwards (from right side to wrong side) into the buttonholes.

SEE ALSO: *Page 290 for button shank.*

Q **Can I fix a button band that seems too heavy for my sweater?**

A Try using a larger hook and correspondingly fewer stitches. If you aren't happy with the results using a single crochet band, you might try the following:

SEED STITCH BAND

ROW 1: Single crochet evenly across, ending with an odd number of stitches.

ROW 2: Ch 1, sc in first stitch, *ch 1, skip next stitch, sc in next stitch; repeat from * across row, turn.

ROW 3: Ch 1, sc in first stitch, *sc in next chain space, ch 1, skip 1 sc; repeat from * across, ending sc in ch-1 space, sc in last sc.

Repeat Rows 2 and 3 as many times as desired, adding buttonholes as desired.

KEY	
○	chain
+	single crochet

seed stitch

Q Is it possible to crochet buttons?

A There are several ways to make a crocheted button. Here are three:

CROCHETED RING BUTTON

1. Leaving a 6" tail, single crochet around a purchased "bone" ring as many times as you can. If you have a big ring, you may need to make an additional round or two of single crochet in order to fill in the interior of the circle.

2. Cut the yarn, leaving an 8" tail. With a tapestry needle, thread the longer tail through the tops of every single crochet around.

3. Pull the threaded yarn tight, bringing stitches to inside of ring.

If necessary, take a couple of stitches across to tighten the center. Use both ends to sew onto button band.

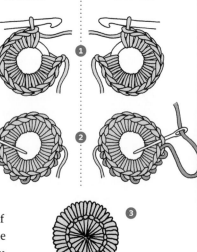

LEFT-HANDED   RIGHT-HANDED

CROCHETED STUFFED BUTTON

Leaving an 8" tail, ch 3, join with slip stitch to first chain (or use an alternate beginning for a tiny center (see page 171).

ROUND 1: Ch 1, 8 sc in ring, join with slip stitch to first sc.

ROUND 2: Ch 1, sc in first stitch, *2 sc in next stitch, sc in next stitch; repeat from * around, omitting last sc, join with slip stitch to first sc. [12 sc]

ROUND 3: Ch 1, sc in each sc, join with slip st to first sc.

ROUND 4: Ch 1, *pull up a loop in next 2 sc, yo and pull through all loops on hook (dec made); repeat from * around, stuffing ball with a length of the same yarn before finishing round. Fasten off and cut yarn, leaving a 10" tail.

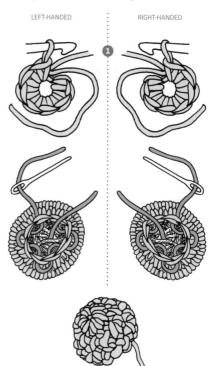

LEFT-HANDED   RIGHT-HANDED

Thread tail through tops of all stitches on last round and pull tight. Thread the 8" tail down through center of button, and use both ends to sew button to fabric.

TINY BALL BUTTON

1. Leaving an 8" tail, ch 2. Sc 7 in second ch from hook. *Do not join.*

2. Make 2 sc in each stitch around. Fasten off. Pull beginning tail to tighten hole and bring tail to inside. Thread ending tail through back loop of each single crochet stitch around.

3. Roll ending tail into a ball to serve as stuffing. Pull threaded tail tight, tacking together as necessary to form ball.

4. Use ending tail to sew to fabric.

LEFT-HANDED · RIGHT-HANDED

288

Q What's the best way to sew on a button?

A Sew it on just the way you would any button, using sewing thread in a color to match your yarn or your button. You can also use colored embroidery floss. Insert the needle from the back of the fabric to the front, up through the button and back down, then back into the fabric. At this point, if you put the needle through the loop made by the beginning knot, you'll prevent the knot from slipping up through the fabric. Make sure the threads are smooth and snug against the button, then continue sewing. When you have made several passes through the button, take a couple of small stitches on the back of the button band and cut the thread.

using a reinforcing button

If your fabric is flimsy or your button will get hard use, you may want to reinforce the stitching by adding a backing, such as another button or a piece of fabric or felt on the wrong side of the fabric. Stitch through the reinforcing button on the wrong side of the fabric as you sew the button on the right side. Thicker fabrics require that you use a button with a shank, or make your own sewn button shank (see next question).

Q How do I sew a button shank?

A A button shank allows space between the button and the fabric to which it is attached. To create a shank, put a toothpick or small crochet hook between the button and the button band to create a space, and begin to sew on the button in the usual way. Before you finish it off, remove your spacer, bring the thread up through the button band, around the loose threads between the button and the band, and back to the wrong side; take a couple of small stitches on the back of the button band, and cut the thread.

making a button shank with a reinforcing button

Q Can I put a crocheted border on my knit sweater?

A Absolutely! Crocheted edges can enhance knit garments. Because crocheted borders are firm and flat, they can serve as a good substitute for knitted edgings, which may curl or stretch out of shape. Crocheted buttonholes are usually an improvement over knit ones, as well.

Start with a crochet hook in a size larger than the needle size you used for knitting. For example, if you used a U.S.

size 7 (4.5 mm) knitting needle, use a 5.0 mm crochet hook. Follow the instructions on page 270 for picking up edge stitches along a crocheted fabric, practicing first on your knit swatch if possible. Crochet stitches usually are wider than their knit cousins, so chances are you won't be picking up one crochet stitch for every knit stitch or row.

CHAPTER 11

The Finish Line

So you're almost finished stitching, but you dread the next step? Although finishing may never be one of your favorite tasks, with the right knowledge you may find it becomes less onerous.

All's Well That Ends Well

Q What is the first step in finishing?

A Starting out right. An important but often overlooked aspect of finishing starts before you first pick up your hook. Knowing what to expect of your fabric and using good technique throughout makes the final finishing steps easier. Use your washed and blocked swatch to practice borders, buttonholes, and any other finishing details.

SEE ALSO: *Pages 155–69 for working a swatch.*

Q Too late. I didn't read that part about blocking my swatch and I've already finished stitching. What do I do now?

A Once again the answer is: "It depends." The finishing methods you choose depend in part on the yarn, the fabric you have made, and the purpose of the finished item. For instance, if you are making a stuffed toy, you can just stuff it and sew it together with no blocking. If you are making a thread doily, on the other hand, you need to wash, block, and starch it. If you are making a garment, you may need to block the pieces before you sew them together, then add edgings or other finishing touches. No matter what the finishing method, the first step is weaving in ends.

Q How do I *weave in ends*?

A There is no one right way to weave in ends. Whatever method secures the ends, works for you, and makes you satisfied is right. The ends don't have to be invisible from the wrong side, but you don't want them slipping to the front of the work to be seen by all and sundry.

Here's one method that works well on most fabrics: Thread a tapestry needle with the yarn tail. (When beginning and ending a yarn, always leave at least a 6" tail, so you'll have an end to work with.) On the wrong side, run the tip of the tapestry needle through the back of several stitches in one direction, then turn and run it through the back of every other stitch in the other direction, or through the back of every stitch on the next row in the other direction. You may need to try a variety of ways to get ends to stay put, depending on your yarn and fabric. If you're working with silk, rayon, or other slippery yarns, you need longer tails that you can weave them diagonally one way and then diagonally in the other direction.

If you have long tails left where you finished a ball and are going to be sewing a seam, you

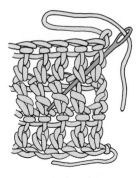

weaving in ends

may leave those alone for now. You can either use those ends for seaming, or work the tails into the seam after it is made.

....

Q **Any tips on threading a tapestry needle? I hate the way the yarn always seems to split when I try.**

A The easy way? Fold the yarn tail over the needle and pinch it up near the needle. Holding your fingers next to the needle, slide the yarn off the pointed end of the needle and insert the folded end into the needle's eye.

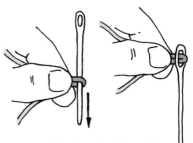

threading a tapestry needle

....

Q **I hate weaving in ends. Is there any way to take care of tails left when starting a new color or ball so that I don't have to worry about them later?**

A Many crocheters like to work over the tail of the old yarn as they work the first few stitches in a new yarn. As you begin a new yarn, hold the tails of yarn to the left (*to the right for Lefties*) along the top of the stitches on the previous row or round. When you insert the hook into the next stitch and pull up a loop, make sure that you are working around the yarn tails, catching and securing them into the fabric as you work each of the next couple of inches of stitches. If you find that this method is too bulky, leave the ends to be woven in later.

One disadvantage of this method is that the ends tend to work themselves out over time. To avoid this, work over the yarn tails for several stitches, then leave a 4" tail free. When the crocheting is finished, go back and weave in those short yarn tails with a tapestry needle as described above.

LEFT-HANDED

RIGHT-HANDED

working in tails as you stitch

Q I'm using a very slippery yarn and finding it particularly difficult to hide the ends, which tend to pop out of the finished fabric. Do you have suggestions?

A The usual method of weaving in ends as you work is less successful with slippery yarns, and it also may not hide contrasting yarns satisfactorily. Some silk and rayon ribbons take any opportunity to slide free. Whenever you're working with these yarns, leave longer ends (8"), so that when the fabric is finished, you can work them diagonally through the back of several stitches one way, and then diagonally in the opposite direction. You could also try tacking down the ends with sewing thread in a matching color. You may find it helpful to put a dot of soft fabric glue on the ends. (Try it first on your swatch to make sure you are happy with the way it feels against your skin.)

Q What if my ends are too short to weave in?

A You can use a crochet hook or latch hook to draw the ends under other stitches. Next time you make something, be more generous with the ends so that you'll have more to work with.

Q How do I weave in ends on a chain?

A This presents a bit more of a problem, since you don't have much there to weave into. With a tapestry needle, go back and forth around the bump on the reverse side of the chain, or try going round and round that bump. Tug the chain a bit before trimming the ends to allow the tails to stretch with the chains. Try different methods to see what works best with your yarn.

SEE ALSO: *Page 77 for back bump of chain.*

Crocheter's Block

Q What is *blocking*? Do I have to do it?

A Blocking is the means by which pieces are shaped to their final measurements, using moisture and sometimes heat. It may be compared to pressing seams open in sewing, but it is not ironing. Blocking sets the stitches and may enhance the drape of the fabric. It can make all the difference between a sweater that is obviously homemade and a quality handcrafted sweater. Blocking makes it easier to work seams and edgings and may enable you to make minor size adjustments. But blocking is not the time to correct size problems caused by inaccurate gauge calculations. It's too late for that! Many crocheted items benefit from a quick dose of steam, and some, such as doilies, require blocking in order to reach their final shape.

Q What materials do I need in order to block?

A Depending on which blocking method you use, you need a yardstick or tape measure; rustproof pins; a steamer, steam iron, or plant mister; water; and some type of water- and heatproof surface that you can pin into. Blocking wires are a nice option for blocking lace.

Q **What kind of work surface do I need?**

A It needs to be large and flat, so that the pieces lie flat without hanging over the edge. An ironing board works for small pieces, but you often need something bigger.

The work space needs to be able to withstand some abuse, as it is subjected to moisture and/or heat, as well as to being stuck with pins. It also needs to remain undisturbed until the blocking is finished. This may take from a few minutes to a day or more, depending on the circumstances. For example, wet cotton can take days to dry in the humid summer season. (Voice of Experience: Cats love warm, steamy fabric. A door that closes securely is a bonus.) The surface also needs to be waterproof and not subject to dye transfer. In other words, make sure your blocking surface won't add color to your crochet, and that your crochet won't add color to your blocking surface.

....

Q **Do I need to buy a special blocking board?**

A No, although having a blocking board made especially for the purpose is a great tool if you have the space to store it. These are available from retailers, or you can make your own from rigid insulation board, cork boards, or interlocking foam floor mats, which can be configured in different shapes to fit your needs. Cover any do-it-yourself blocking boards with colorfast towels or cotton cloth.

. . . .

Q If I don't have a blocking board, what should I do?

A You can use a spare bed, a carpeted corner of a room, a large sofa cushion, or a piece of foam rubber. Cover it with a waterproof layer, such as an old shower curtain or trash bag, topped by a couple of layers of towels or blankets. Be sure the towels are old so their colors won't bleed onto your work. (Voice of Experience: Count the number of pins you use and be sure to collect them all when you finish. You don't want to share your bed, carpet, or sofa with large straight pins.)

. . . .

Q Is there more than one way to block?

A You can choose among three basic methods, based on the fiber content of your yarn and your own preference:

▶ **Wet blocking,** for fibers that can tolerate plenty of water

▶ **Cold blocking,** for fibers that can tolerate dampness but not heat

▶ **Steam blocking,** for fibers that can tolerate damp and heat (the quickest method)

Q Which blocking method should I use?

A Look at your yarn label; it may indicate the best blocking method for that yarn. If different fibers have been combined in the same item, choose the method appropriate for the most delicate fiber. Most animal fibers (wool, mohair, alpaca) tolerate steaming. Plant fibers like cotton and linen can be wet-blocked. Some man-made fibers can be ruined (the technical term is *killed* — truly) by too much heat, so wet or cold blocking is best for those. Novelty and metallic yarns may not be suitable for any type of blocking.

. . . .

Q How does *wet blocking* work?

A Wash or thoroughly wet the pieces, then squeeze out excess water. Do not wring or twist! Place pieces face down on the blocking surface and pat into shape. Use a yardstick to make sure the pieces are the size you want. Check to be sure that each sleeve is blocked to the same dimension. Pin onto the blocking surface at each corner and at approximately 2"–3" intervals along

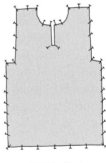

wet blocking

edges. (Voice of Experience, emphatic: Make sure your pins are rustproof. Rust stains do not come out.) Allow the items to dry. If you are impatient, you can set up a fan to blow over the surface to hasten drying.

. . . .

Q What's the procedure for *cold blocking*?

A Place the dry pieces on the blocking surface as for wet blocking, and pin along each edge. Check your measurements, and make sure that the rustproof pins are close enough together so they don't distort the fabric. Spritz the pieces with clean water until they are damp. Allow them to dry.

. . . .

Q How do I *steam block*?

A Measure and pin the dry pieces as for wet blocking. Fill a steam iron or steamer with water, and use the "steam" setting. Hold the iron no closer than 1" over fabric, and allow steam to work into fabric. Move the iron as needed to cover entire fabric. *Do not press or allow the iron to touch the fabric.* Leave undisturbed until pieces are cool and completely dry.

Q How do I use blocking wires?

A Carefully thread a blocking wire through each straight edge of your crocheted piece without piercing the yarn. If the edge is straight, thread the wire in and out through every other row of selvedge stitches; if the edge is scalloped or pointed, insert the wire through the tips of the points or scallops. Arrange one blocking wire in a straight line on your blocking surface and pin it in place, inserting the pins at equal distances next to the blocking wire (not in the actual fabric) and smoothing and stretching the fabric to the desired finished dimensions as necessary. Once the first side is straight, continue pinning the other blocking wires in turn, taking care to check for right angles and straight edges.

Q What's the recommended way to block three-dimensional pieces?

A Wet blocking may be the best bet. Get the pieces damp, then stuff them with rolled-up plastic grocery bags or other waterproof material. If the piece is round, fill it with an inflated balloon. Leave it undisturbed until it is dry. You can put a hat on a wig stand.

Q How do I block a doily?

A Doilies, snowflakes, and other lacy thread crochet items sometimes come off the hook looking a bit like a rag, but careful blocking brings out their beauty. To ensure that your points are symmetrical, prepare a template for the piece by drawing the desired shape on a piece of paper. Cover the paper with plastic wrap or wax paper, and place it on your blocking board. If you are going to starch the piece, do so now (see next question). Otherwise, wash or wet the item thoroughly, then pin it onto the template using rustproof pins. You may need to stretch it a bit. Start by pinning opposite sides and the major points, then pin out scallops or any other special shaping. Allow it to dry thoroughly. You may find it helpful to copy and enlarge the sample doily blocker shown here.

sample doily blocker

Q How do I stiffen thread crochet?

A Whether and how you stiffen your thread crochet item depends on its intended use. Three-dimensional items like baskets may require a permanent hard finish, while doilies may look better with a softer hold. Some methods result in a permanent hold, while others must be reapplied with each washing. When you select your starch, keep in mind that some turn yellow with age and many are not resistant to moisture.

▶ **Spray starch.** Although spray starch gives a weak hold, it's easy to apply and is appropriate when you want to use it to add just a bit of body to a piece. To stiffen with spray starch, prepare a template and pin the item to it to block, as described for doilies (or other items) above. Spray on starch when pieces are pinned out but still wet.

▶ **Liquid starches.** For each of the following methods, prepare the mixture, dip piece(s) in mixture to wet thoroughly, and squeeze out excess. Block as described above.

Powdered or liquid starch. Follow mixing directions on the container. You can make the item stiffer, if desired, by using a higher concentration of starch than directed.

Sugar starch. Boil together equal parts sugar and water until syrupy. Allow to cool slightly. This is an old-fashioned method and easy to do, but it may attract ants. In addition, sugar-starched items may wilt in high humidity.

Cornstarch. Mix 6 parts water to 1 part cornstarch (or a different proportion, depending on your needs). Cook over medium heat until thickened. Allow to cool slightly. This method also wilts in highly humid conditions.

continued on next page >>

Glue. Mix well equal parts white glue and water. As with sugar starch and cornstarch, dampness can be a problem with glue-starched items.

There are several other commercial stiffening products on the market, each with different holding properties. Follow instructions on the container.

．．

Q Blocking sounds like too much trouble. Do I always have to do it?

A No. Some things really are fine without any blocking at all. Some three-dimensional pieces might be difficult to handle, certain fibers may not be suitable for blocking, and very small items such as Christmas ornaments may not need it at all. Some acrylics do best with a simple trip through the washer and dryer. However, most natural fibers, garments, and anything that needs to be seamed benefit from a good blocking.

Joining Motifs

Q My afghan squares aren't all the same size. Is there anything I can do about it?

A Oops! If you notice the problem right away, before you finish stitching, check to be sure you are following the instructions correctly and that you didn't accidentally change hook sizes. If the squares are done in different stitch patterns, however, you may have to use a different hook size for each stitch pattern in order for all the squares to come out the same size.

If you notice the problem after you've made all of your squares, maybe you can block them to match. Blocking can sometimes accomplish small size changes, but don't count on brute force and a bit of steam to make a 10" square into a 12" square. Instead, try working an extra round or two on the smaller squares to bring them up to size. If just a few squares are larger than the others, perhaps you can take out a round or two to bring them into line, or restitch the large ones on a smaller hook.

. . . .

Q How do I join separate motifs?

A You have a lot of choices here. Your joining method is dependent on the look you want and on the type of stitch you used on the last round of your square. Do you want the join to be part of the overall design, or do you want it to be invisible, or almost so? Stitching the final round of each square in the same color makes invisible joining easier. A single crochet seam on the right side, on the other hand, makes the join a decorative element.

If specific joining instructions are not given in your published pattern or if you want a different look to your finished project than the original, experiment with each of the options listed below to determine which one looks best with your project. No matter which method you use, check from time to time to make sure you are working at the correct tension. The seams or joins should have a similar feel and fluidity to the rest of the fabric.

▶ Wrong sides together, whipstitch through both loops.

▶ Wrong sides together, whipstitch through inside loops only.

▶ Wrong sides together, slip stitch or single crochet through both loops.

▶ Wrong sides together, slip stitch or single crochet through inside loops only.

▶ Right sides together, single crochet through both loops.

whipstitching through inside loops only

SEE ALSO: *Pages 316–17 for slip stitch and single crochet seams.*

▶ Use a zigzag chain or chain-and-skip seam.

▶ Join motifs as you go (JAYGo)

SEE ALSO: *Page 310 for join-as-you-go techniques;* Connect the Shapes Crochet Motifs *(see page 396) for more joining methods.*

Q How do I work a *zigzag chain*?

A There are various ways to use chain stitches as decorative joins. Here is a zig-zag chain that can be adapted to a number of situations:

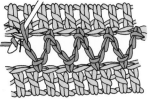

zigzag chain join

Working with square pieces, arrange the squares in the desired pattern. Slip stitch or single crochet in the corner of one square to join yarn, chain 3, then slip stitch or single crochet into the second or third stitch from the corner of the adjacent square. Continue to alternate slip stitches or single crochets and 3-stitch

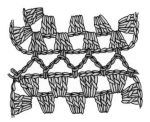

zigzag join for granny square

chains back and forth between the squares, skipping one or more stitches between each joining stitch.

Q How do I work a chain-and-skip seam?

A This is another useful and decorative seam that can be adapted by chaining and skipping the appropriate number of stitches for the situation. With right or wrong sides together as desired, single crochet through both loops of both pieces, chain 2, skip 2 stitches, sc through the next pair of stitches. Continue connecting the pieces with single crochet stitches separated by a short chain over the skipped stitches.

. . . .

Q How do I join motifs as I go?

A The join-as-you-go (JAYGo) method works best when the final round of each motif has a lacy or openwork edge. If you are working from a published pattern, the instructions may explain how to join the motifs as you work. If you don't have finishing instructions, look at your motifs and see how they fit together. Draw a diagram so you can see where the motifs touch. Do they meet at certain points only or do they touch along the entire edge? If they touch along the entire edge, you may choose to join them in every stitch, or only to join them in every other stitch, or some other interval that seems appropriate for the design.

For a basic JAYGo project, complete one motif. Work the next motif up to the final round; then on the final round, work to the spot where the motifs should touch. Insert the hook into the first motif at the corresponding connection point (possibly a chain space); work a joining stitch to join the two motifs, then continue to work the final round of the current motif, joining to the previous motif at appropriate points in the same manner. There are several choices for joining stitches; experiment, then choose the best one for your situation.

....

Q How do I join motifs with a slip stitch?

A This is a fast and easy join that brings the pieces up very close to one another. The slip stitch sits on top of and dominates the stitch it is worked into.

1. Work to the point where you need to join the current motif to the previous motif.

2. Insert the hook from front to back (right side to wrong side) in the stitch or space of the previous motif at the point where you want them to meet.

3. Yarnover and pull up a loop through everything on your hook to complete the slip stitch, then continue working the next stitch on your current motif.

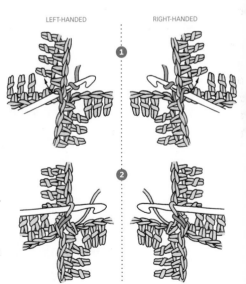

LEFT-HANDED   RIGHT-HANDED

Q How do I make a single crochet join?

A This join is a bit larger and more visible than the slip
stitch join, and it allows a bit of space between the pieces.

1. Work to the point where you need to join the current
motif to the previous motif.

2. Insert the hook from front to back (right side to wrong
side) in the stitch or space of the previous motif at the point
where you want them to meet.

3. Yarnover and pull up a loop, yarnover and pull through
two loops to complete the single crochet.

4. Continue working
the next stitch on
your current
motif.

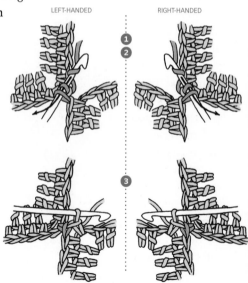

LEFT-HANDED   RIGHT-HANDED

Q How do I make a flat join?

A If you prefer a more invisible connection between the two motifs, try a *flat join*. Work to the joining point on the current motif, drop the loop from the hook and insert hook from front to back (right side to wrong side) into the corresponding connection point on the previous motif. Pick up the dropped loop and pull it through everything on the hook, then continue working the next stitch on your current

motif. This is a quite beautiful and easy join that brings the pieces close together yet keeps the two pieces in balance; neither side of the join dominates the other.

LEFT-HANDED   RIGHT-HANDED

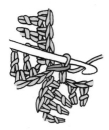 

Other Joining Stitches

Q How do I make a whipstitch seam?

A This is the most common way of sewing a seam in crochet. Thread a tapestry needle with yarn. Holding pieces with right sides together, insert the needle from front to back through both layers of fabric and pull the yarn through. Take care to work under the strands of yarn without splitting them. Work close to the selvedge when working along a vertical edge; on a horizontal edge, you may choose to work under one or two loops of the V.

whipstitch seam

Q What is *mattress stitch*?

A Mattress stitch is a type of seam done using a tapestry needle and working on the right side of the fabric. After all, that's the side that needs to look good, so you want to be able to keep an eye on how the seam is shaping up. Working from the right side makes matching stripes or stitch patterns a breeze.

MATTRESS STITCH

1. Hold the pieces to be joined with right sides facing up, side-by-side and parallel to each other. Clip or pin the pieces together. Use a blunt-tip tapestry needle and a length of the same yarn you stitched with. If you have a long tail left over at one corner from the foundation chain, begin with that. If you are starting a new yarn, leave a 6" tail to be woven in later, but don't knot the yarn.

2. Insert the needle vertically under and out of a stitch on one piece and then under and out of a stitch exactly opposite on the other piece. As you insert the needle, do not split the yarn of the stitch you are working into, but work under a strand of yarn within the stitch; exactly which strand of yarn will vary based on the selvedge stitch. Moving up a row on the first piece, stitch under a strand of yarn in the next stitch on that side, then under a corresponding strand in a stitch on the second piece. Do this a couple of more times on each side, then tug gently on the working yarn to pull the two pieces together. Don't pull too hard, just hard enough to get them to sit next to each other.

3. Continue stitching back and forth between the pieces and snugging them together every so often for the length of the seam. When the seaming is complete, weave in the ends of the seaming yarn.

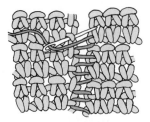

mattress stitch

Q How do I handle mattress stitch with different kinds of stitches?

A When you are joining single crochet fabric, you'll probably go into every stitch on each side. If you are working with a double or treble crochet fabric, you may need to put a stitch into the side of each post as well as at the top or bottom of the stitch. When using a fancy or openwork pattern stitch, experiment to discover the best place to put your seaming stitches. If you are joining fabrics with different types of stitches along their edges, use your judgment and check from time to time to make sure the pieces are aligned correctly.

. . . .

Q How do I slip stitch pieces together?

A This is usually done on the wrong side of the fabric. Hold the pieces to be joined with right sides together. Insert the hook all the way through both edge

stitches. Yarnover and pull through a loop. *Insert the hook into the next pair of stitches and pull up a loop through both layers of fabric and on through the first loop on hook; repeat from * until the entire length is joined. Slip stitch seams can be tight and unforgiving. As you work, stop and examine what you've done to ensure that you have maintained an even tension. If your seam is too tight, you may need to use a larger hook than the one you used on the garment.

. . . .

Q How do I single crochet pieces together?

A This is similar to making a slip stitch seam, but you work single crochet instead of slip stitch. The seam is bulkier yet more flexible than a slip stitch seam. The seam will be on the wrong side if worked holding right sides of the pieces together. If worked with wrong sides together, the seam becomes a decorative element on the right side.

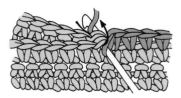

. . . .

Q Why don't my pieces fit together evenly?

A Count your rows or stitches to make sure they are the same on each piece to be joined. If not, can you add or remove a row or two? Did your gauge change? Try sewing the pieces from the right side, matching row for row.

You may be able to block them to the same size, or possibly adjust which rows/stitches you are joining a bit when you sew them together to make a better match. (Just a little adjusting here: Don't try to hide a 2" difference, as a buckling seam is sure to give away your secret!)

Tender Care

Q How do I clean my finished piece?

A Now that you've spent all that time making your gorgeous crocheted project, you'll want it to last a long time. When you made your swatch, you read the care instructions on the yarn label, and then washed and blocked your swatch as appropriate for the fiber content, so you know what to expect. Before you launder your handiwork, take a look to see that buttons and any embellishments are secure, and that no ends are coming loose. (Voice of Experience: Some buttons cannot be laundered; others cannot be dry-cleaned. You may need to remove these before washing or dry-cleaning.)

Machine wash. If you can machine-wash and -dry your item, by all means do so. Use the gentle cycle and low heat. Many machine-washable yarns need to be machine-dried as well to regain their elasticity.

Hand-wash fabrics by using tepid water and a small amount of gentle soap or detergent. Put the item into the sudsy water and gently squeeze the lather through the fabric.

Rinse well. Squeeze out excess water gently. Do not wring or twist! Now you have two options for removing excess water:

▶ Pick up the wet item carefully, supporting its weight, and lay it flat between two clean towels. Roll the item and towels together, and squeeze to blot out the excess water.

▶ Put the wet item into the washing machine, and run a gentle spin cycle for a few moments. Finish by laying the piece flat to dry.

Dry cleaning is a good option for novelty yarns and others labeled "dry clean only." (Voice of Experience: Some yarns labeled "dry clean" can be carefully hand-washed. If you suspect yours can be hand-washed, try washing a swatch.)

SEE ALSO: *Page 388 in appendix for yarn care symbols.*

Q How should I store crocheted items?

A Clean them first; body oils attract dirt that appears like magic when items are put away and makes wool more attractive to moths. Fold crocheted items, if possible, and store them in a dark, dustproof container. If the item is going to be stored for a long time, refold it from time to time to avoid permanent creases that might weaken the fabric. Some items can be wrapped around a wrapping-paper tube instead of being folded; use acid-free tissue paper to keep the item from directly touching the cardboard, and between layers of the fabric. Use a moth repellent for animal fibers or blends.

CHAPTER 12

Something (Not Quite) Completely Different

Up to this point, we've talked about the basics of crocheting and following patterns. Now it's time to sample some extras that can enhance your newly found knowledge. If you are intrigued by what you read in this section, find out more in To Learn More, page 390.

Tunisian Crochet

Q What is *Tunisian crochet*?

A This crochet technique is worked with a long-handled tool called an afghan hook, which looks like a cross between a knitting needle and a crochet hook. Some Tunisian hooks have a long cable on one end to allow wider widths than would be possible with a straight hook. There are also interchangeable hook/cable sets that allow you to use an assortment of cable lengths and hook sizes. Tunisian crochet combines elements of both crochet and knitting. Individual Tunisian simple stitches are square, making them an ideal base for cross-stitch embellishment.

afghan hook

Q What are the basics of Tunisian crochet?

A Tunisian crochet is made with a combination of forward passes and return passes, also known as forward and return (or reverse) rows. Each combination of a forward pass and return pass creates one Tunisian crochet row. The forward pass is worked from right to left (*left to right for Lefties*) and loads up the hook with stitches; the return pass is worked from left to right (*right to left for Lefties*) and binds off the stitches. Unlike many crochet stitches, there is a clear right and wrong side to the fabric; it is worked with the right side facing you at all times. When choosing a hook size, it is best to go up several sizes from the size you would normally use for a particular yarn, in order to keep the fabric supple. Tunisian Simple Stitch (TSS) is the most common pattern.

....

Q How do you work Tunisian Simple Stitch (TSS)?

A This is the stitch also commonly known as afghan stitch. With an afghan hook, chain as many stitches as you need for the width of your piece.

1. **Foundation Forward Pass.** Insert hook in second chain from hook and pull up a loop as you would for single crochet. Leave that loop on the hook, and pull up another loop in the next chain. Continue on down the chain, pulling up a loop in each chain and leaving it on the hook. Do not turn the work. You should end with as many loops on the hook as you had chains.

NOTE: *Another option is to work into the back bump of the chain (page 77) for a more finished look.*

2. Return Pass. Yarnover and pull through first loop on hook (the equivalent of a turning chain), *yarnover, and pull through 2 loops on hook; repeat from * across row. You now have one loop on the hook, which counts as the first stitch of the next row.

3. Forward Pass. Holding hook in front and inserting it from right to left (*left to right for Lefties*) throughout, insert hook under front of vertical bar of the next-to-last stitch in the previous row and pull up a loop, *insert hook under vertical bar of next stitch and pull up a loop; repeat from * across row. Do not turn the work.

4. Continue working steps 2 and 3 for the Tunisian Simple Stitch, ending with a return pass.

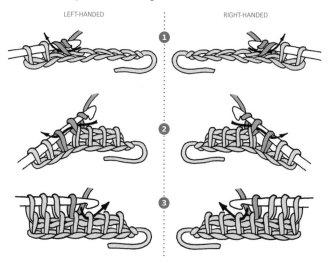

LEFT-HANDED   RIGHT-HANDED

5. Bind off. Work a slip stitch row as follows: *Insert hook under next vertical bar and pull up a loop, pulling the loop all the way through the loop on hook, so that one loop remains on hook; repeat from * across row.

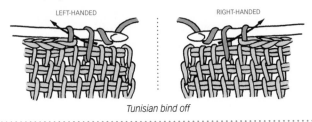

LEFT-HANDED   RIGHT-HANDED

Tunisian bind off

Q How do I work Tunisian Knit Stitch (TKS)?

A Work the foundation chain, a foundation forward pass, and a return pass as for Tunisian Simple Stitch. Then continue as follows:

FORWARD PASS: Holding hook in front and inserting hook from front to back between the two vertical bars (front and back) of the stitches throughout, insert hook between the front and back vertical bars of the next-to-last stitch in the previous row, pull up a loop, *insert hook between the vertical bars of next stitch and pull up a loop; rep from * across.

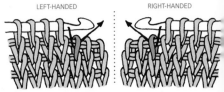

LEFT-HANDED   RIGHT-HANDED

TKS forward pass

RETURN PASS: Work as for Tunisian Simple Stitch.

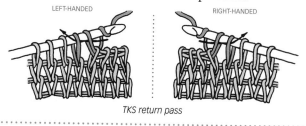

LEFT-HANDED   RIGHT-HANDED

TKS return pass

Q What is Tunisian Reverse Stitch (TRS)?

A This one is a bit tricky at first, but it's a great stitch to use to help combat curl, especially in the first few rows of a piece. Work the foundation chain, a foundation forward pass, and a return pass as for Tunisian Simple Stitch.

FORWARD PASS: Holding the yarn and hook in back, and inserting hook from right to left (*left to right for Lefties*) under the back vertical bar throughout, insert hook under the back vertical bar of the next-to-last stitch in the previous row. Pull up a loop. * Insert hook under the back vertical bar of next stitch and pull up a loop; repeat from * across.

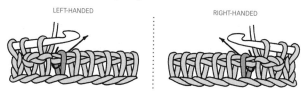

LEFT-HANDED   RIGHT-HANDED

TRS forward pass

RETURN PASS: Work as for Tunisian Simple Stitch.

LEFT-HANDED   RIGHT-HANDED

TRS return pass

Q What is Tunisian Purl Stitch (TPS)?

A This is another stitch that takes a bit of practice, but it's a basic stitch worth learning because it also combats curl. Work the foundation chain, a foundation forward pass, and a return pass as for Tunisian Simple Stitch.

FORWARD PASS

1. Holding the yarn in front, and inserting hook from right to left (*left to right for Lefties*) under the front vertical bar as for Tunisian Simple Stitch throughout, insert hook under the front vertical bar of the next-to-last stitch in the previous row.

LEFT-HANDED   RIGHT-HANDED

2. Yarnover by allowing the working yarn to come in front of the vertical bar; then under, around, and over the hook; pull the yarnover up through the bar; *insert hook under the front vertical bar of next stitch and pull up a loop as described above; repeat from * across.

RETURN PASS: Work as for Tunisian Simple Stitch.

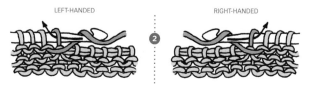

LEFT-HANDED · RIGHT-HANDED

Q **Can I work other stitch patterns in Tunisian crochet?**

A Absolutely! You can make all kinds of fabrics, including Tunisian double stitch (like double crochet), rib, basket weave, bobbles, lace, clusters, and a variety of other stitches. You can increase, decrease, and otherwise shape pieces. You can do beautiful color work or lace work. You can combine Tunisian with regular crochet and with knitting as well.

Q My Tunisian fabric is curling forward. How do I prevent that?

A There are several tricks you can try:

▶ Use a larger hook than you might expect, perhaps 2 to 5 sizes larger than you would ordinarily use for that size yarn.

▶ Keep your tension relaxed.

▶ Work the foundation chain loosely, and work the foundation forward pass into the back bump of the chain.

▶ Use a variety of stitch patterns. Worked alone, Tunisian Simple Stitch and Tunisian Knit Stitch tend to curl forward, but you can combine them with Tunisian Reverse Stitch, Tunisian Purl Stitch, or other stitch patterns to mitigate the curl.

▶ Block the fabric, according to the fiber.

▶ Add a crocheted edging wide enough to tame the curl.

▶ Work in different directions, with some sections headed up and down, and others headed sideways, as in a Log Cabin–style afghan.

SEE ALSO: *Pages 298–306 for blocking; pages 268–76 for edgings.*

Q How do I decrease in Tunisian crochet?

A When working a forward pass, insert the hook under the next two (or more) vertical bars and pull up one loop. You may also simply skip one stitch when working a forward pass, although this may leave an unsightly hole.

. . . .

Q How do I increase in Tunisian crochet?

A Pick up an extra loop at any point by inserting the hook from front to back under the horizontal strand that goes between two vertical bars. A yarnover on the forward pass adds a stitch, but it also creates a hole, which may or may not be desirable.

. . . .

Q How can I tidy my edges?

A There are several things you can do to create nice smooth selvedges. If the edge that starts the forward pass (the near edge) is loose compared to the edge that starts the return pass (the far edge), make sure that you are allowing the last loop of each forward pass to reach the full diameter of the hook shank, rather than snugging down into the throat, and loosen up on the first chain of the return pass. To tame a loose near edge, give an extra tug to tighten the first stitch you pick up on the forward pass, when there are still just two loops on the hook.

In Tunisian Simple Stitch, the near edge has a nice column of chains marching up the side, while the far edge doesn't sport that nice chained look. To create a chained selvedge on the far edge, insert the hook under both the last vertical bar of the forward pass *and* under the semivertical strand that lies next to it.

. . . .

Q **What projects are best suited to Tunisian crochet?**

A Most people associate Tunisian crochet with afghans. (After all, another name for the Tunisian simple stitch is "afghan stitch.") Accessories and garments can be made with afghan stitch, as well. The length of the hook limits the width of the fabric, however, so wide pieces must be worked on a hook with an extended cable, or worked in narrower pieces, then seamed.

Other Kinds of Crochet

Q What is *double-ended crochet*?

A Double-ended crochet is a type of Tunisian crochet worked with a long, double-ended hook. It is usually done with two contrasting colors and makes a thick fabric perfect for afghans, potholders, and so on. The tool and technique are also known as cro-hook or Crochenit hook.

. . . .

Q How do I work double-ended crochet?

A There are many different stitches possible when working double-ended crochet. Here's just one, a variation of Tunisian Simple Stitch (TSS):

double-ended hook

DOUBLE-ENDED CROCHET

Using a double-ended hook and two contrasting-color yarns, begin by chaining the number of stitches needed for your desired width with Color A. Note that you are still working a forward pass and a return pass, yet with two colors of yarn. In the instructions below, each of these passes is labeled a "row."

ROW 1: Pick up a loop in each chain as for TSS. Drop color A, but do not cut it.

LEFT-HANDED   RIGHT-HANDED

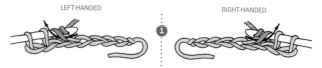

ROW 2: Turn the work and push it to the other end of the hook. With Color B, work a Return Pass as for TSS. Do not turn.

LEFT-HANDED   RIGHT-HANDED

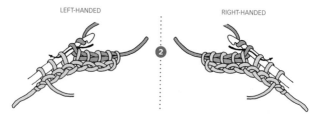

ROW 3: With Color B, work a Forward Pass as for TSS. You'll be working under the vertical bar formed by Color A. Count to see that you've maintained the same number of stitches. Drop Color B.

LEFT-HANDED   RIGHT-HANDED

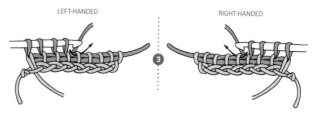

ROW 4: Turn the work and push it to the other end of the hook. With Color A, work a Return Pass as for TSS.

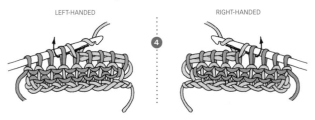

LEFT-HANDED   4   RIGHT-HANDED

ROW 5: With Color A, work a Forward Pass as for TSS, working under the vertical bars formed by Color B. Count your stitches again.

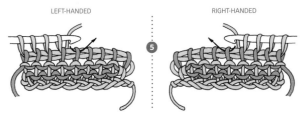

LEFT-HANDED   5   RIGHT-HANDED

Repeat Rows 2–5 until desired length. Finish off with a Tunisian bind-off.

NOTE: *As you finish each pair of rows, the yarn you need to pick up will be waiting for you at the beginning of the row. There are many variations of this simple double-ended stitch. Go learn more!*

Q How can I keep track of where I am in double-ended crochet?

A If you are lost, take a look at where you are, what's on your hook, and what needs to happen next. You'll see that you are working two rows of each color. The first row of each color starts when the hook is full of stitches in the other color and ends with just a single stitch on the hook. The second row of each color loads up the hook again with stitches. Turn the hook at the end of every other row, when it is full of stitches and a new color is about to begin.

Q What is *thread crochet*?

A Thread crochet is crochet made with very smooth yarn with a narrow diameter, called thread. The thread is most commonly made of cotton, although there are silk and linen threads as well. The thread may be fine, requiring a small steel hook. Thread crochet is most often used to make doilies, lace, and filet stitch patterns.

Q Are there any special tips for thread crochet?

A With most threads you'll be using a steel hook that tapers from the tiny head up to the thumb rest. Unlike regular crochet hooks, where you make the stitch on the shank (the fattest part of the hook before the thumb rest), in thread crochet you may need to make the stitches on the tapered section. This is because, with the smallest hooks, the thumb rest/handle section has to be larger than the working diameter in order to be strong enough to withstand use, as well as large enough for you actually grab and manipulate.

Look for the long "sweet spot" of the taper, and draw all the loops up to that spot to maintain an even tension.

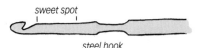

sweet spot

steel hook

Most threads are made of inelastic fiber, so to avoid getting hand cramps, take care not to clench the yarn or hook too tightly. You'll probably want to work your foundation chain on a slightly larger hook than the rest of the piece. You are looking for a fabric in which the stitches are neither so tight that you can't insert your hook into them nor so loose that they look sloppy; it may take some practice to find just the right tension.

. . . .

Q **How is *Irish crochet* different from any other crochet?**

A Irish crochet is a type of thread crochet that results in beautiful three-dimensional lace. It was developed in Ireland to mimic the more expensive European needle laces. Floral motifs are worked individually, then joined with a mesh or filling stitch to form the lace fabric. Traditionally,

continued on next page >>

stitches in the motifs were worked over a cord to pad and add dimension to the stitches. Modern crochet borrows certain techniques and motifs from Irish crochet, and we tend to call any thread crochet involving flowers "Irish crochet." Thread flower and leaf motifs on mesh backgrounds are a bow to the traditional Irish techniques.

. . . .

Q What is *Clones lace*?

A Clones lace is a type of Irish crochet, named after the village in which it originated and was marketed. A special feature of Clones lace is the Clones knot, which is used both in the mesh filling stitch and in individual motifs. There are several variations of a Clones knot. Here's one to try:

1. Chain several stitches, pulling out the last stitch to make an elongated chain that will be the base of the knot.

2. * Yarnover, pass the hook from front to back under the chain, yarnover and pass the hook from back to front under the chain.

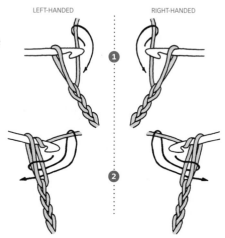

LEFT-HANDED   RIGHT-HANDED

3. Repeat from *
several more times
until the elongated
chain is covered by
the stitches
wrapped onto the
hook; yarnover and
pull through all the
loops on the hook.

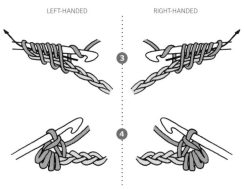

LEFT-HANDED

RIGHT-HANDED

4. Single crochet
in the chain just
before the elongated chain. Chain several
more before working the next Clones knot.

SEE ALSO: *Page 390,* To Learn More

Q What is *filet crochet*?

A In filet crochet, double crochet and chain stitches are
arranged to form a grid or *ground* of blocks and spaces.
Filet crochet often
depicts letters and
pictures, and is
often worked in
thread. When you
work a pattern, the
pictures and motifs

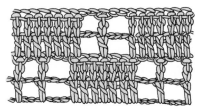

filet crochet

are presented as graphs. The example shown here is a simplified version of a technique that often results in an intricate and beautifully lacy fabric.

. . . .

Q What kind of hook and thread or yarn should I use for filet crochet?

A You can use any size thread or yarn you like; the size of the thread will determine the size of the grid. The smaller the thread/yarn, the more detail you can incorporate into your design. Use an appropriate-size hook for your chosen thread/yarn.

. . . .

Q How do I read a filet crochet graph?

A Each square in a filet crochet chart represents either a *block* (a.k.a. *solid mesh*) that is filled with double crochets or a *space* (a.k.a. *mesh*) that is created by chain stitches. A filled-in block usually represents three double crochet stitches (one side of the block, plus two "fill-in" stitches), while an empty space signifies a double crochet and two chain stitches

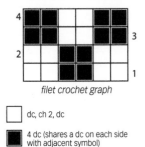

filet crochet graph

☐ dc, ch 2, dc

■ 4 dc (shares a dc on each side with adjacent symbol)

(one side of the block, plus two "empty" stitches). Adjacent blocks and spaces share a common double crochet stitch. In addition, there is a double crochet at the end of the row to balance the pattern. When working a block over a space, work the two center double crochets into the chain-2 space, rather than into the chain stitches themselves.

Start at the bottom right-hand corner of the chart (*bottom left-hand corner for Lefties*). Follow the first row from right to left (*left to right*); follow the second row from left to right (*right to left*).

. . . .

Q How do I know how many to chain for a filet crochet foundation?

A To determine the number of stitches you need for the foundation chain, count the number of squares across the bottom row of the graph and multiply that number by three. Next, note whether the beginning square of the first row is a block or a space. If it's a block, add 3 chains to your starting chain to count as the first double crochet of the block. If the first square is a space, add 5 chains to your starting chain to count as a chain-3 dc plus a chain-2 mesh.

For example: (6 blocks × 3) = 18 for foundation chain

18 + 5 = 23 chains to start (foundation chain + first dc and ch-2 space of first row).

Some patterns have you add an extra stitch for the foundation chain, to allow the first ch-3 "double crochet" to sit on a ch-1 foundation. This makes a slightly squarer corner. If you prefer, you can chain a total of 24 to begin the sample, then work the first dc in the 9th chain from the hook.

. . . .

Q Can you spell it out for me?

A Sure. Pick up your yarn and hook and try it out, using the sample filet crochet graph above. Here's the symbol crochet version of that graph, without the extra foundation chain.

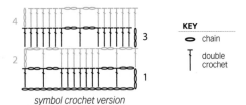

KEY

○— chain

Ⱦ double crochet

symbol crochet version

Here's the text version of the sample graph:

Chain 23.

ROW 1: Dc in 8th ch from hook, ch 2, skip 2 ch, dc in next ch, dc in next 6 ch, (ch 2, skip 2 ch, dc in next ch) two times, turn.

ROW 2: Ch 5 (counts as dc plus ch-2), dc in next dc, ch 2, dc in next dc, dc in next 6 dc, (ch 2, dc in next dc) two times, ending with last dc in top (3rd ch) of turning chain, turn.

ROW 3: Ch 3 (counts as dc), (2 dc in next ch-2 space, dc in next dc) two times, (ch 2, skip 2 dc, dc in next dc) two

times, (2 dc in next ch-2 space, dc in next dc) two times,
ending with last dc in top of turning chain, turn.

ROW 4: Ch 3 (counts as dc), dc in next 6 dc, (ch 2, dc in next
dc) two times, dc in next 6 dc.

. . . .

Q **What other symbols might I see on a filet graph?**

A Two other common features of filet graphs are *lacets*
(a.k.a. *fancy* mesh) and *long meshes* or *double space*. A
lacet is a type of filet crochet stitch that adds a curve to the
normally gridlike filet. It is stitched as "dc in next dc, ch 3,
skip 2 sts or chains, sc in next
st or ch, ch 3, skip 2 sts or
chains, dc in next dc."

A long mesh is simply a
rectangular space created by
putting two mesh spaces
together without a double
crochet stitch between them;
in other words, a chain-5 space.

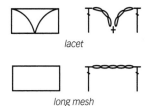

lacet

long mesh

Q Is a *Solomon's Knot* hard to make?

A A Solomon's Knot, also known as a *Love Knot* or *Lover's Knot*, is an unusual stitch made from a series of long chains and single crochet stitches. It is often used by itself to form an attractive openwork mesh, but it can be used in combination with other crochet stitches. The length of the extended loop will vary based on your yarn weight and the pattern instructions. It takes some practice, but once mastered it is fun and fast to do.

SOLOMON'S KNOT

1. Begin with a slip knot on the hook. Ch 2, single crochet in second ch from hook.

2. Loosen the loop on the hook until it is about ¾"–1" long. Yarnover and pull through the loop on the hook, but do not allow the working yarn or extended loop to

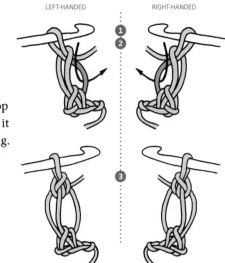

LEFT-HANDED

RIGHT-HANDED

tighten. Take a moment to identify the back bump of the extended chain you just made; it's between the double strand of yarn on the right (*left for Lefties*) and the single strand of yarn on the left (*right*). Insert the hook under the back bump, between the double and single strands.

3. Single crochet into this strand (yarnover and pull up a loop, yarnover and pull through two loops).

Repeat steps 2 and 3 until you have as many Solomon's Knots as you desire.

SOLOMON'S KNOT MESH

FOUNDATION ROW: Work an even number of Solomon's Knots, ending with step 3 above. Each extended loop/sc combination counts as 1 "knot."

ROW 1: Skip 3 long loops, sc in next sc, (2 Solomon's Knots, skip 2 loops, sc in next sc) across, turn.

ROW 2: 3 Solomon's Knots, skip 4 long loops, sc in next sc, (2 Solomon's Knots, skip 2 loops, sc in next sc) two times, turn.

Repeat row 2 for Solomon's Knot Mesh.

LEFT-HANDED

RIGHT-HANDED

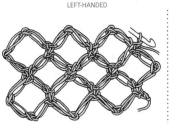

Q How do I work *broomstick lace*?

A Broomstick lace is worked with one very large knitting needle (U.S. size 17 or 19, as big as a broomstick!) and a crochet hook. It is similar to Tunisian crochet in that it is worked with right side facing and there are two steps needed to complete each row; the first step loads up the knitting needle with a series of loops that are worked off in the second step. As with most stitch patterns, there are many variations; individual patterns will give you specific instructions.

BASIC SINGLE CROCHET BROOMSTICK LACE SWATCH

SETUP ROW (RS): Ch 17. Sc in the second chain from hook and in each chain across. Do not turn. [16 sc]

ROW 1: Elongate the loop on the hook until it is large enough to fit over the knitting needle; place the loop on the needle. Working from left to right (*right to left for Lefties*), *insert the hook into the next sc, yarnover, pull up a loop and place the loop on the needle; repeat from * across. At the end of the row you should have 16 loops on the needle. Do not turn.

ROW 2: * Insert the hook from right to left (*left to right for Lefties*) into the next 4 sts together, yarnover and pull up a loop through all 4 sts, dropping the loops from the needle, ch 1 (counts as first sc), place 3 more sc in the center space of these 4 loops; repeat from * across. Do not turn. Repeat Rows 1 and 2 for stitch pattern.

LEFT-HANDED

RIGHT-HANDED

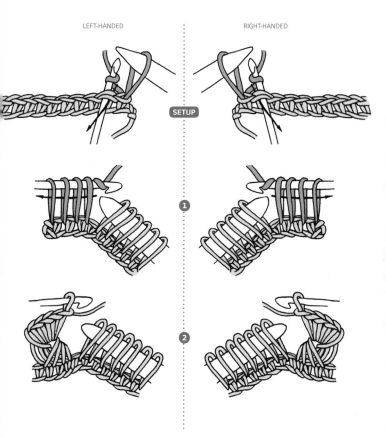

SETUP

1

2

Q **Does it matter which way I put the stitches on the needle?**

A Yes, it does matter. In general you insert your hook under closest loop first, from right to left (*left to right for Lefties*). If you insert your hook starting with the farthest loop on the needle, your group of loops will be twisted, which could be used as a design element. But be consistent.

. . . .

Q **What is hairpin lace?**

A Hairpin lace, or hairpin crochet, is made with a crochet hook and a special handheld loom or "fork." Series of loopy strips are crocheted onto the fork, and the resulting strips may then be connected to create an openwork, lacy fabric. The size of the loops is determined by the distance between the side prongs; most looms allow you to adjust this width. As with many crochet techniques, there are plenty of variations too numerous to cover here!

BASIC HAIRPIN LACE STRIP

Holding the loom with the removable bar at the bottom, make a slip knot and slide it onto the left prong (*right prong for Lefties*). Slide the knot toward the right (*left*) so that it is equidistant from each prong and creates an elongated loop. Note that you will be working stitches into the left-most (*right-most*) loop throughout.

1. Wrap the yarn from front to back over the right (left) prong, then back to the left (right) side. From here on out, tension the yarn in your non-dominant hand as you do for ordinary crochet. Insert the hook from bottom to top through the loop on the left (right) prong, yarnover, and pull through the loop, then chain 1.

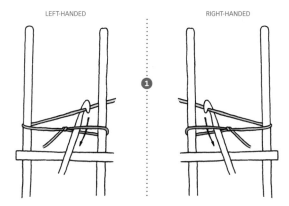

LEFT-HANDED

RIGHT-HANDED

2. Rotate the hook so that the handle is in the 1:00 o'clock (11:00 o'clock) position, and slip the handle behind the right (left) prong. Now turn the loom as you would turn the page of a book to read the next (previous) page.

3. After turning, the hook is now on the front of the loom and the yarn has wrapped around the right (left) prong. Insert the hook from bottom to top under the *front* strand of the left-hand (right-hand) loop; yarnover, pull up a loop, yarnover, pull through two loops to complete a single crochet.

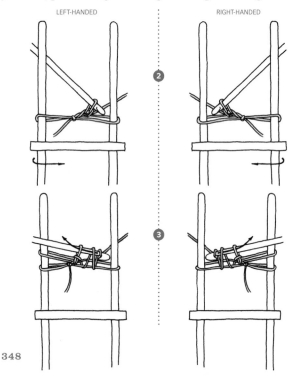

LEFT-HANDED

RIGHT-HANDED

Repeat Steps 2 and 3 to fill the loom with loops, remembering to turn the loom the same way each time and keeping the stitches centered in the middle of the loom. As the loom fills, remove the bar and allow the completed stitches to slide off, then replace the bar to continue the strip. (If you slip the stitches from the loom onto two pieces of waste yarn, the waste yarn will keep the free loops from tangling.)

LEFT-HANDED   RIGHT-HANDED

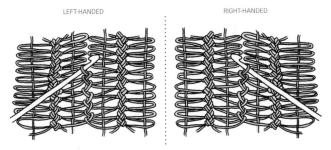

Make sure you have completed the same number of loops on each side. After completing the last loop, insert the hook from top to bottom through the back of the right (left) loop — the loop opposite the one you just worked — yarnover and pull through the loop on the hook. Fasten off.

. . . .

Q How do I join the completed strips?

A To join strips using the cable method, hold strips parallel. Insert hook from front to back into first loop on the right (*left*), then into first loop on the left (*right*), pull left loop through right loop (*right through left*). Insert hook into next loop on right (*left*) and pull through, then continue to alternate sides until all loops have been joined. Using the yarn tail from one of the strips, yarnover and pull through a loop (that is, chain 1 with the yarn tail). Fasten off.

· ·

Q **What is *free-form crochet*?**

A It's fun! Free-form crochet is a completely pattern-free way of crocheting. Indeed, to do it properly, you *can't* have a plan. Use scraps of yarn and a variety of stitch patterns and shapes to paint a textural fabric. Hard to explain, but easy to do!

Using a yard or two of yarn, crochet a little piece in any shape, in any stitch pattern that suits you. Increase and decrease willy-nilly to create a free-form shape. We're not talking squares here, but little pieces that move. Do only a few rows/rounds, then fasten off the first yarn. Add on to the first piece with other yarns in your choice of coordinating colors, picking up stitches from the edge of the existing piece. Your free-form motif can be any size or shape. If you are trying to make a particular shape (such as for a purse or a vest), you may have to crochet a few extra pieces to fit your puzzle, but that's the only time you should have to plan. This is a technique that unleashes your artistic side! Mix a variety of yarns, weights, and colors to create a unique fabric.

Q **What do crocheters do with their free-form pieces?**

A You can do anything you chose. Use tiny free-form shapes as brooches or embellishments. Use larger free-form pieces to make vests, coats, afghans, pillows, or wall hangings. If you are shaping a garment, use large paper or newsprint to make a full-sized template of each garment piece you need. Make smaller free-form pieces (6 to 8 square inches each) and place them on your template, then fill in the spaces as necessary to create your desired shape.

Q **Is there anything I should be cautious about with free-form crochet?**

A Not really, because there are no rules. You can choose your palette carefully, or mix colors in wild abandon. You will have a lot of ends to weave in, however.

Q **My first tries at free-form crochet are very rippled. How can I get them to lie flat?**

A Are you sure you want them to be flat? Free-form crochet is just that. Three-dimensionality, including bumps and ripples, can be part of the beauty of the design. However, if you don't like the results you are getting, review the guidelines in chapter 6 about making round motifs lie flat, and those in chapter 10 about making flat edges.

Q How do I make *Bruges lace*?

A Crocheted Bruges lace imitates a type of needle lace originally from Bruges, Belgium. In Bruges lace, crochet a straight "tape" of double crochet stitches flanked by chain spaces, then curve and shape the tape by gathering and connecting the chain-space loops in beautiful patterns. Here's a sample of the technique:

BRUGES LACE CURVE

Chain 10.

ROW 1: Dc in 7th ch from hook and in next 3 ch, turn.

ROWS 2–11: Ch 6, dc in next 4 dc, turn.

ROW 12: Ch 6, dc in next 4 dc.

ROW 13: Ch 3, insert hook into next 3 chain spaces along edge of tape, yarnover and pull up a loop through all three spaces to slip stitch them tightly together, turn, ch 3, dc in next 4 dc.

ROW 14, 16 AND 18: Ch 6, dc in next 4 dc.

ROW 15, 17 AND 19: Ch 3, slip st in next free loop of tape, turn, ch 3, dc in next 4 dc, turn.

Bruges lace

Q Can I combine crochet with knitting?

A Great idea! Some items are better knitted than crocheted, and vice versa. Three-dimensional items are easier to crochet than to knit. Knitted fabric's flexibility means that it may be better suited for sweaters and garments, but crocheted garments work well if you take care to create a suitable fabric. Because crochet can be less flexible and is more likely to lie flat, it is a wonderful choice for edging your knitted sweaters. Knitted ribbing hugs better than crocheted ribbing, so try knitted cuffs on your next pair of crocheted mittens. Tunisian crochet is a kind of mix of knit and crochet, so see what happens when you mix all three together in one project. Use your imagination, and you'll think of dozens of other ways to combine the two.

Baubles and Beads

Q How are beads measured?

A Beads are measured in either millimeters or *aught* sizes. Common seed beads are measured in aught sizing, using a number and a degree symbol, as 6°, or a number/zero, as 6/0. While millimeter sizing is straightforward, the aught sizing is a bit more confusing because the larger the number, the smaller the bead. An 11° bead is smaller than a 6° bead, which is smaller than an 8°. Beads from different countries and from different manufacturers may have different qualities and sizes, even when they have the same size designation.

. . . .

Q How do I choose the correct size bead?

A The beads need to complement the crocheted fabric and be large enough to enhance the design without being so large that they overpower it or make the fabric too heavy. The hole in the bead should accommodate the yarn without abrading it.

You'll want to experiment with your chosen beads before making a commitment. Not all beads of the same size have the same size hole, so you may find you need to choose a different bead or a different type of bead to work with a particular yarn. In general, 11° beads will work with size 20 crochet thread and laceweight yarns; 6° beads will work with size 10 crochet thread and fingering-weight yarns; and 8° will work with DK- and sport-weight yarns. Worsted-weight yarns require larger beads, although you may find some 8° seed beads that will accommodate a light worsted weight yarn.

Q How do I add beads to my crochet?

A There are several different beading techniques for crochet, enough for another book or two! Here are several:

METHOD #1

String the beads onto your yarn before you begin to crochet. (See page 360 for advice on how to do this.) You'll have to plan ahead to know how many beads you need and if you are using a color pattern, you'll have to string them in order, from the last bead used to the first. The beads wait near your yarn ball until you're ready for them. When you work them in, they show on the back side of the stitch; therefore your beading row is always a wrong side row. The bead will sit vertically on the stitch.

FOR SINGLE CROCHET:

▶ Work to the spot where you want to insert a bead; insert hook into stitch and pull up a loop; pull a bead up so that it is next to the hook, then yarnover and pull through both loops on hook (A).

▶ You can also pull up beads between single crochet stitches (B).

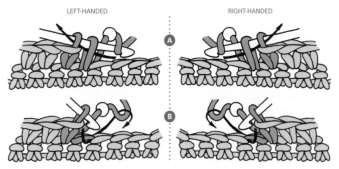

LEFT-HANDED   RIGHT-HANDED

beading with single crochet

FOR DOUBLE CROCHET:

▶ Complete the first "yarnover, insert hook and pull up loop" (A), pull a bead up next to the hook, then complete the double crochet stitch.

▶ You can also pull up beads before the final "yarnover, pull through 2 loops" (B).

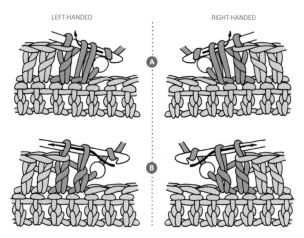

LEFT-HANDED   RIGHT-HANDED

A

B

beading with double crochet

METHOD #2

This method requires that you have a crochet hook that will fit through the hole of the bead, plus some ease. In many cases, this will be a tiny beading hook, much smaller than the hook you are using to crochet with. You don't have to plan ahead with this technique, as you will be placing beads individually, as needed. The bead will sit horizontally on the right side.

Crochet in pattern to the point where you want to place the bead. Drop the loop from your hook, insert the beading hook through the bead and draw the dropped loop through the hole in the bead to hoist the bead up onto the fabric. Place the dropped loop back onto your working hook and continue working.

METHOD #3

Make loops of beads for fringe, by pulling up many beads together and allowing them to hang from the front of the fabric before working the next stitch.

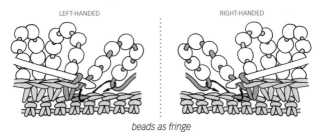

LEFT-HANDED   RIGHT-HANDED

beads as fringe

Q My beads don't show. What did I do wrong?

A There are a couple of possibilities:

▶ You may have worked them in on a right-side row, with a method that places the beads on the back of the work. Try working them in on wrong-side rows only.

▶ The beads may be too small to show up on your fabric; try slightly larger beads.

▶ If your yarn is fuzzy or highly textured, the beads may be hidden by the yarn. Try larger beads or a different yarn.

▶ Clear beads or beads in a color that closely match the yarn color will present more as texture and glimmer rather than as individually recognizable beads.

Q How do I string beads onto my yarn?

A You may use a specially designed threader called a Big Eye threader, or use a do-it-yourself, multipurpose threader. Here's how:

1. Thread a 6" length of sewing thread onto a sewing needle. Tie the ends together in a tight overhand knot.

2. Place the end of the yarn into the loop formed by the thread.

3. Using the sewing needle, pick up several beads at a time and allow them to fall down the needle and thread to the yarn.

4. With your fingers, carefully pull the beads down over the spot where the yarn and the thread cross, then down onto the yarn.

Continue picking up beads and sliding them onto the yarn until all the beads are picked up.

Q How do I make yarn *fringe*?

A Cut lengths of yarn twice the length you want your finished fringe to be, plus 1 or 2 inches. You need the extra length to allow for the knot and for a bit to be trimmed off. Holding 3 or more strands together, fold them in half to form a loop. Insert a crochet hook from the wrong side to the right side of the edge of the fabric and pull through the loop made by the folded strands. Draw the ends of the fringe through the loop and tug gently to tighten the knot.

attaching fringe

Q My fringe looks pitiful. What's wrong?

A Don't be stingy with your yarn! Good fringe takes lots of yarn. Use lengths that are long enough to be in proportion to your crocheted item, use enough strands in each bundle, and place the bundles close enough together to give a luxurious look. Thin yarn can make thin fringe; use lots of yarn or use a different yarn for the fringe. Take care to always insert the hook from the same side of the fabric so that the fringe knots end up on the same side.

Some yarns don't hold up well for fringe. Test your yarn's hardiness and suitability for fringe by holding a few strands together and running your hands down past the ends of the yarn, squeezing a bit as you do so. Do this several times. Now shake the ends. Are they starting to look ragged? Did you harvest large bits of fuzz when you ran your hand over the yarn? If so, you may want to choose another yarn for fringing, or to omit the fringe altogether.

. . . .

Q Is it "pompom" or "pompon"? And how do I make one?

A Either term is correct. Start with either a commercial pompom maker or cut out two doughnut-shaped cardboard disks as shown for a homemade pompom maker. The pompom will be slightly smaller than the outside diameter of your disks.

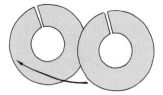

pompom maker

MAKING A POMPOM

1. Holding the disks together, wrap yarn through the center and around the outside of both pieces until you can't fit any more yarn through the center hole — or until you can't stand wrapping any more! (Voice of Experience: You'll be tired of this process long before you are finished, but keep wrapping.)

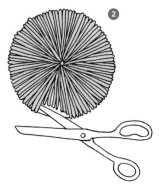

2. Using sharp scissors and holding the center of the pompom maker carefully, cut along the outer edge of the disks, making sure the bottom blade of the scissors is between the two disks, as if you were cutting along the groove of a yo-yo. Don't separate the disks yet!

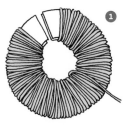

3. Take a 10" long piece of yarn, and wrap it tightly around the center of the pompom bundle, between the two disks. Tie a knot, leaving enough of a tail on each end to sew the pompom onto the item you've crocheted.

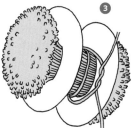

4. Fluff pompom with your fingers, and trim it, if necessary.

Q How do I make a *tassel*?

A Tassels are easier than pompoms!

MAKING A TASSEL

Cut a piece of strong cardboard ½"–1"
longer than the desired length of your
tassel. (If you can find a book about the
right size, use that as your template.)
Next, cut a 4"–7" length of yarn and
place it across the top of the template.
This will be the hanging loop.

1. Wrap yarn lengthwise around the
template as many times as needed to get
the desired thickness. Tie the hanging
loop securely around the top of the tassel.
Cut yarn at base of cardboard.

2. Slide the wraps and hanging loop
carefully off the template.

3. Cut an additional length of yarn about
2½ times the length of the tassel. Wrap
this piece tightly around all the strands,
¼"–1" from the hanging loop. Secure the
ends of the wrapping yarn by threading
them under the wraps and down through
the center of the tassel. Trim the ends.

Q How do I make a *twisted cord*?

A Also known as a *monk's cord*, this popular cord is simple for even non-crocheters.

MAKING MONK'S CORD

1. Cut three or more strands of yarn at least 3 times the desired finished length. Place an overhand knot at each end of the bundle of yarn. Put a crochet hook or pencil into one end to act as a handle. Slip the other end over a hook or door-knob. (Voice of Experience: Even better, get someone to help you hold one end. Kids love to do this!)

2. Using the "handle," twist the yarn until it is tight. You may have to move a little closer to the stationary end as you twist, but keep some tension on it and hold on! As it twists, it tends to jump out of your hands and kink up.

3. Pinch the yarn at the halfway point and bring the knotted ends together, allowing the cord to twist on itself.

4. Carefully untie the knots, and retie each end with an overhand knot.

If you like, you can make tassels at each end of the cord by tying a knot several inches from each end and allowing the ends to unravel.

. . . .

Q **What is a surface chain, and how do I do it?**

A A surface chain is simply a crocheted chain (or slip stitch) that is worked onto the front of a fabric (crocheted, woven, or knitted) to give the look of chain-stitch embroidery. Holding the yarn on the wrong side of the fabric, insert the hook from front to back into the fabric, yarnover and pull up a loop through the fabric and through the loop on the hook. Continue inserting the hook from front to back into the fabric at equal intervals and pulling up a loop, creating the desired pattern.

The length of the chain and placement of the stitches is up to you. Work horizontal lines, vertical lines, or free-form curves. At the end of the chain, cut the yarn, leaving a 6" tail, bring the yarn tail to the right side, through the last loop on the hook, then back again over the last chain loop to the wrong side to secure the last stitch of the chain. Weave in the end.

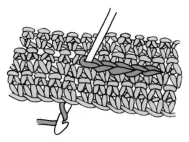

Appendixes

Standard Crochet Abbreviations

SYMBOL	ABBREVIATION	TERM/EXPLANATION
	() OR [] OR {}	Work instructions within parentheses/brackets as many times as directed
	*	Repeat instructions following asterisk as many times as directed
	**	Repeat instructions between asterisks as many times as directed, or repeat directions from a certain point, or end last repeat of directions at this point
	A, B, C, etc.	Colors A, B, C, etc.
	alt	alternate/alternating; every other
	beg	begin, begins, beginning
	bet	between
⌒	BL; blo	back loop(s); back loop(s) only Loop away from you at top of stitch
⊥	BPdc	back post double crochet
⊥	BPhdc	back post half double crochet
	CC	contrasting color
●	ch(s)	chain stitch, chain(s)

SYMBOL	ABBREVIATION	TERM/EXPLANATION
	ch-sp	Chain-space (ch- followed by a number refers to a specific chain space)
	CL	cluster
	cont	continue
dc symbol	dc	double crochet
dc2tog symbol	dc2tog	double crochet two together
	dec	decrease(s), decreasing
dtr symbol	dtr	double treble crochet
edc symbol	edc	extended double crochet
ehdc symbol	ehdc	extended half double crochet
esc symbol	esc	extended single crochet
etr symbol	etr	extended treble crochet

SYMBOL	ABBREVIATION	TERM/EXPLANATION
⌣	FL, flo	front loop(s); front loop(s) only
	FPdc	front post double crochet
	FPhdc	front post half double crochet
	FPsc	front post single crochet
	FPtr	front post treble crochet
	hdc	half double crochet
	hk	hook
	inc	increase, increasing
	LH	Left hand
	lp(s)	loop(s)
	MC	main color
	mult	multiple
	patts OR pat(s)	pattern(s)
	pm	place marker
	prev	previous

SYMBOL	ABBREVIATION	TERM/EXPLANATION
	rem	remain, remains, remaining
	rep	repeat(s)
	RH	right hand
	rnd(s)	round(s)
	RS	right side
+ OR ✕	sc	single crochet
✕✕	sc2tog	single crochet 2 together
	sk	skip
	sl	slip
•	sl st	slip stitch
	sp(s)	space(s)
	st(s)	stitch(es)
	tch OR t-ch	turning chain
	tog	together
![treble crochet symbol]	tr	treble crochet, triple crochet
	WS	wrong side
	Yo; yoh	yarnover; yarnover hook

Common Crochet Terms and Phrases

THIS PHRASE	MEANS
above markers	Measure from where markers were placed.
at the same time	You are going to be doing two or more things at once. For example, neckline and shoulder shaping often occur at the same time.
attach/join new yarn	Begin working with a separate ball of yarn, either the same color or a different color.
back, front	Beginning with lowercase letters, *back* and *front* usually mean the work as you hold it. The back of the stitch is the side away from you; the front is the side closest to you.
Back, Left Front, Right Front, Left Shoulder, etc.	These are the names of sweater pieces as they are worn. The left shoulder is the part that will be on the wearer's left shoulder. If you have trouble remembering which piece you are working on, hold it up to your body and see which way it fits. *Hint*: Sweater piece names are often capitalized.
ball band/ yarn band	The identifying label on each ball or skein of yarn. It contains information on fiber content, weight, yardage, care instructions, and suggested hook sizes.
block	Blocking is a very important step in making your garments look professional, and it can solve a multitude of problems. See the index for references in the book about blocking.

THIS PHRASE	MEANS
body of sweater is worked in one piece to underarm	Just what it says. You start with enough stitches for the front and back of the sweater at the same time, and work it as one piece until you divide for the armhole openings.
continue in this manner	Keep on doing whatever you've been doing: increasing, decreasing, working in stitch pattern, whatever the preceding instructions have said.
ease	The difference between the wearer's body measurement and the finished sweater measurement. Ease is necessary for a good fit, but it varies according to the style of sweater.
end off/fasten off	After the last stitch is worked, pull working yarn through last stitch to secure it.
end with WS row (or RS row)	The last row that you work is a WS row (or RS row).
finished measurements	The measurements of the project after blocking and seaming
join	Connect end of one round with beginning of same round, usually with a slip stitch.
keeping to pattern, keeping in established pattern . . .	While doing whatever shaping is about to be described, keep working the stitch pattern as you have been, making adjustments for a change in stitch count so that the pattern stitch remains uninterrupted.

THIS PHRASE	MEANS
. . . or size needed to obtain gauge	Change hook sizes until you get the gauge called for in the pattern. If your first attempt results in too many stitches per inch, increase your hook size. If you get too few stitches per inch, decrease your hook size.
post	Vertical part of a stitch.
pull up a loop	Wrap yarn around hook and pull it through fabric. This term is usually preceded by "insert hook in stitch/fabric/etc. and . . ."
reverse shaping OR reversing shaping	You are probably working a cardigan front and have worked one side. On the other side, you need to work the neckline and armhole shaping on the opposite side from the piece you just worked.
Right Side, Wrong Side	These are the names for the "public" and "private" sides of a piece.
RS facing/ WS facing	The side that you are about to work is the right side (or wrong side) of the fabric.
schematic	A graphic representation of a finished project, showing finished dimensions
selvage st/ selvedge st	A stitch at the beginning/end of a row that will be used for seaming or other finishing. It is not part of the pattern stitch. Not all patterns contain selvage stitches, and many that do contain them do not identify them as such.

THIS PHRASE	MEANS
sizes: S (M, L, XL) [S (M, L, XL)]	Patterns usually give several sets of measurements. The first set may be for children and the second set for adults, or the first for women and the second for men; the pattern instructions explain. Determine which size you want to make and circle or otherwise mark it throughout the pattern.
stitch multiple	The number of stitches used to complete a repeat of a pattern. For example, a stitch multiple of 8 plus 3 would mean that the pattern is worked on a multiple of 8 stitches, plus 3 extra/selvage stitches. Thus, it could be worked over 19 sts, 27 sts, 35 sts, and so on.
swatch	A small piece of stitching used to determine gauge, fabric hand, washing results, finishing techniques. Swatches are crucial in almost every project. They can tell you much more than just what your gauge is going to be. Take time to learn to do them well.
tapestry needle	A large, blunt-tip yarn needle

Standard Body Measurements & Sizing

The following is reprinted from *Standards & Guidelines for Crochet and Knitting* (April 2003), with permission of the Craft Yarn Council. See www.yarnstandards.com.

Most crochet pattern instructions provide general sizing information, such as the chest or bust measurements of a completed garment. Many patterns also include detailed schematics or show specific garment measurements (chest/bust, neckline, back, waist, sleeve length, etc.) in all the different pattern sizes. To ensure proper fit, always review all of the sizing information provided in a pattern before you begin.

Following are several sizing charts. These charts show Chest, Center Back Neck-to-Cuff, Back Waist Length, Cross Back, and Sleeve Length body measurements for babies, children, women, and men. These measurements are given in both inches and centimeters.

When sizing sweaters, the fit is based on actual chest/bust measurements, plus ease (additional inches or centimeters). The first chart entitled "Fit" recommends the amount of ease to add to body measurements if you prefer a close-fitting garment, an oversized garment, or something in between.

The next charts provide average length for children's, women's, and men's garments.

Both Fit and Length charts are simply guidelines. For individual body differences, changes can be made in body and sleeve lengths when appropriate. However, consideration must be given to the project pattern. Certain sizing changes may alter the appearance of the garment.

HOW TO MEASURE

CHEST/BUST. Measure around the fullest part of the chest/bust. Do not draw the tape too tightly.

CENTER BACK NECK-TO-CUFF. With arm slightly bent, measure from back base of neck across shoulder around bend of elbow to wrist.

BACK WAIST LENGTH. Measure from the most prominent bone at the base of the neck to the natural waistline.

CROSS BACK. Measure from shoulder to shoulder.

SLEEVE LENGTH. With arm slightly bent, measure from armpit to cuff.

FIT

VERY CLOSE-FITTING: Actual chest/bust measurement or less

CLOSE-FITTING: 1"–2" (2.5–5 cm)

STANDARD-FITTING: 2"–4" (5–10 cm)

LOOSE-FITTING: 4"–6" (10–15 cm)

OVERSIZED: 6" (15 cm) or more

LENGTH FOR CHILDREN

WAIST LENGTH: Actual body measurement
HIP LENGTH: 2" (5 cm) down from waist
TUNIC LENGTH: 6" (15 cm) down from waist

LENGTH FOR WOMEN

WAIST LENGTH: Actual body measurement
HIP LENGTH: 6" (15 cm) down from waist
TUNIC LENGTH: 11" (28 cm) down from waist

LENGTH FOR MEN

Men's length usually varies only 1–2" (2.5–5 cm) from the "back waist length" measurements (*see chart on page 382*).

Standard Body Measurements & Sizing

BABY'S SIZE		3 MO.	6 MO.	12 MO.	18 MO.	24 MO.
CHEST	in.	16	17	18	19	20
	cm	40.5	43	45.5	48	50.5
CENTER BACK NECK-TO-CUFF	in.	10½	11½	12½	14	18
	cm	26.5	29	31.5	35.5	45.5
BACK WAIST LENGTH	in.	6	7	7½	8	8½
	cm	15.5	17.5	19	20.5	21.5
CROSS BACK (SHOULDER TO SHOULDER)	in.	7¼	7¾	8¼	8½	8¾
	cm	18.5	19.5	21	21.5	22
SLEEVE LENGTH TO UNDERARM	in.	6	6½	7½	8	8½
	cm	15.5	16.5	19	20.5	21.5

CHILD'S SIZE		2	4	6	8	10
CHEST	in.	21	23	25	26½	28
	cm	53	58.5	63.5	67	71
CENTER BACK NECK-TO-CUFF	in.	18	19½	20½	22	24
	cm	45.5	49.5	52	56	61
BACK WAIST LENGTH	in.	8½	9½	10½	12½	14
	cm	21.5	24	26.5	31.5	35.5
CROSS BACK (SHOULDER TO SHOULDER)	in.	9¼	9¾	10¼	10¾	11¼
	cm	23.5	25	26	27	28.5
SLEEVE LENGTH TO UNDERARM	in.	8½	10½	11½	12½	13½
	cm	21.5	26.5	29	31.5	34.5

WOMAN'S SIZE		X-SMALL	SMALL	MEDIUM	LARGE
BUST	in.	28–30	32–34	36–38	40–42
	cm	71–76	81–86	91.5–96.5	101.5–106.5
CENTER BACK NECK-TO-CUFF	in.	27–27½	28–28½	29–29½	30–30½
	cm	68.5–70	71–72.5	73.5–75	76–77.5
BACK WAIST LENGTH	in.	16½	17	17¼	17½
	cm	42	43	43.5	44.5
CROSS BACK (SHOULDER TO SHOULDER)	in.	14–14½	14½–15	16–16½	17–17½
	cm	35.5–37	37–38	40.5–42	43–44.5
SLEEVE LENGTH TO UNDERARM	in.	16½	17	17	17½
	cm	42	43	43	44.5

WOMAN'S (CONT.)		1X	2X	3X	4X	5X
BUST	in.	44–46	48–50	52–54	56–58	60–62
	cm	111.5–117	122–127	132–137	142–147	152–158
CENTER BACK NECK-TO-CUFF	in.	31–31½	31½–32	32½–33	32½–33	33–33½
	cm	78.5–80	80–81	82.5–84	82.5–84	84–85
BACK WAIST LENGTH	in.	17¾	18	18	18½	18½
	cm	45	45.5	45.5	47	47
CROSS BACK (SHOULDER TO SHOULDER)	in.	17½	18	18	18½	18½
	cm	44.5	45.5	45.5	47	47
SLEEVE LENGTH TO UNDERARM	in.	17½	18	18	18½	18½
	cm	44.5	45.5	45.5	47	47

MAN'S SIZE		SMALL	MEDIUM	LARGE	X-LARGE	XX-LARGE
CHEST	in.	34–36	38–40	42–44	46–48	50–52
	cm	86–91.5	96.5–101.5	106.5–111.5	117–122	127–132
CENTER BACK NECK-TO-CUFF	in.	32–32½	33–33½	34–34½	35–35½	36–36½
	cm	81–82.5	84–85	86–87.5	89–90	91.5–92.5
BACK WAIST LENGTH	in.	25–25½	26–26½	27–27½	27½–27¾	28–28½
	cm	63.5–64.5	66–68	68.5–70	70–70.5	71–72.5
CROSS BACK (SHOULDER TO SHOULDER)	in.	15½–16	16½–17	17½–18	18–18½	18½–19
	cm	39.5–40.5	42–43	44.5–45.5	45.5–47	47–48
SLEEVE LENGTH TO UNDERARM	in.	18	18½	19½	20	20½
	cm	45.5	47	49.5	50.5	52

Head Circumference Chart

	PREMIE	BABY	TODDLER	CHILD	WOMAN	MAN
		INFANT/CHILD			ADULT	
in.	12	14	16	18	20	22
cm	30.5	35.5	40.5	45.5	50.5	56

For an accurate head measure, place a tape measure across the forehead and measure around the full circumference of the head. Keep the tape snug for accurate results.

Shoe Size Chart

Infant's & Child's Shoe Size Chart

CHILD'S SIZE (U.S. SIZES)		0–4	4–8	7–11	10–2	2–6
SOCK SIZE (U.S. Sizes)		4–5	5–6½	6–7½	7–8½	8–9½
AGES		6–12 mo.	1–3 y.	3–5 y.	5–9 y.	7–13 y.
11a. FOOT CIRCUMFERENCE	in.	4½	5½	6	6½	7
	cm	11	14	15.5	16.5	17.5
11b. SOCK HEIGHT	in.	2½	3½	4½	5½	6½
	cm	6.5	9	11.5	14	16.5
11c. TOTAL FOOT LENGTH	in.	4	5	6	7½	8
	cm	10	13	15.5	19	20.5

Woman's Shoe Size Chart

WOMEN'S SIZE (U.S. SIZES)		3–6	6–9	8–12
SOCK SIZE (U.S. Sizes)		7–9	9–11	10–12
11a. FOOT CIRCUMFERENCE	in.	7	8	9
	cm	17.5	20.5	23
11b. SOCK HEIGHT	in.	6½	7	7½
	cm	16.5	17.5	19
11c. TOTAL FOOT LENGTH	in.	9	10	11
	cm	23	25.5	28

Man's Shoe Size Chart

MEN'S SIZE (U.S. SIZES)		6–8	8½–10	10½–12	12½–14
SOCK SIZE (U.S. Sizes)		10	11	12	14
11a. FOOT CIRCUMFERENCE	in.	7	8	9	10
	cm	17.5	20.5	23	25.5
11b. SOCK HEIGHT	in.	7	7½	8	8½
	cm	17.5	19	20.5	21.5
11c. TOTAL FOOT LENGTH	in.	9½	10½	11	11½
	cm	24	26.5	28	29

Suggested Sizes for Accessories and Household Items

The following measurements give you a starting point for designing your own accessories and household items.

AFGHANS come in all sizes and shapes. Here are a few typical sizes, but feel free to experiment with other sizes. If you have big folks in your family, you may want to make larger afghans to cover those long legs and big feet! See below for standard U.S. bed sizes. *Note:* Afghan measurements usually exclude fringe.	39" × 60" *(99 × 152 cm)* 40" × 56"–60" *(102 × 142–152 cm)* 43" × 60" *(109 × 152 cm)* 45" × 65" *(114 × 165 cm)* 48" × 60" *(122 × 152 cm)* 46" × 68" *(117 × 173 cm)* 50" × 64" *(127 × 163 cm)*
LAP RUGS AND THROWS are somewhat smaller than afghans, but again, they can be any size that works for you. Throw-size blankets are a good size for kids.	27" × 34"–36" *(68.5 × 86–91.5 cm)* 30" × 30" *(76 × 76 cm)* 37" × 50" *(94 × 127 cm)* 45" × 45" *(114 × 114 cm)*

BEDDING: Different countries have different standard bed sizes. The following measurements are typical for mattresses in the United States; if you are in a different country, you may have a slightly different-size mattress.	Crib	27¼" × 51⅝" *(69 × 131 cm)*
	Twin	39" × 75" *(99 × 191 cm)*
	XL Twin	39" × 80" *(99 × 203 cm)*
	Full/ Double	54" × 75" *(137 × 191 cm)*
	Queen	60" × 80" *(152 × 203 cm)*
	King	76" × 80" *(193 × 203 cm)*
	California King	72" × 84" *(183 × 213 cm)*

BABY BLANKETS are smaller still. Make items for premies even smaller.	**BABY BLANKET:** 25" × 32" (64 × 81 cm), 32"–36" square (81–91.5 cm square) 32" × 40" (81 × 101.5 cm) **CRIB BLANKET:** 36" × 54" (91.5 × 137 cm), 40" × 60" (101.5 × 152 cm)
PILLOWS may be made to fit purchased pillow forms. Typical pillow form sizes are listed at right.	12"–30" square (30.5 × 76 cm square), in 2" (5 cm) increments 6"–7" × 14" (neckroll) (15.5–17.5 × 36.5 cm) 12", 14", 16" circles (30.5, 35.5, 40.5 cm) 26" square (66 cm) (Euro) 27" (68.5 cm) or larger (floor pillows)

FASHION SCARVES can be very skinny (3"/8 cm wide), although most are 4"–6" (10–15 cm) wide. They can be as short or long as you choose, depending on your taste and how much yarn you have.

WARM SCARVES are another matter and need to be long enough to wrap comfortably around the neck and tie or tuck into a coat. Width is important — too wide and it's hard to wear, too narrow and it's not warm enough. For adults, 7"–9" (17.5–23 cm) wide by 58"–72" (147–183 cm) long is usually good. Children need narrower, shorter scarves, about 6"–7" (15–18 cm) wide by 45"–50" (114–127 cm) long.

SHAWLS AND STOLES are about 20" (50.5 cm) wide by 72"–80" (183–203 cm) long, depending on the height of the wearer. Triangular shawls need to be wide enough to stay wrapped around the shoulders. This depends on the size of the wearer, but may be 62"–80" (158–203 cm) wide across the hypotenuse. The length from center-back to tip is usually in the range of 32"–40" (81–101.5 cm).

POTHOLDERS are usually about 7" (18 cm) square;
DISHCLOTHS AND WASHCLOTHS about 9" (23 cm) square.
PLACEMATS are 12" × 16"–18" (30.5 × 40.5–45.5 cm).

Yarn Care Symbols

Symbol	Description	Symbol	Description
	Machine wash		Do not tumble dry
	Hand wash		Iron dry
	Do not wash		Iron, high heat
	Do not bleach		Iron, medium heat
	Tumble dry, normal		Iron, low heat
	Tumble dry, delicate		Do not steam
	Line dry		Do not iron
	Flat dry		Dry clean
	Do not dry		Do not dry clean

Hook Inventory

METRIC	U.S.	
.60 mm	14 steel	☐
.75	14 steel	☐
.85	13 steel	☐
1.00	12 steel	☐
1.1	11 steel	☐
1.25		☐
1.3	10 steel	☐
1.4	9 steel	☐
1.5	8 steel	☐
1.65	7 steel	☐
1.75, 1.8	6 steel	☐
1.9	5 steel	☐
2.0	4 steel	☐
2.1	3 steel	☐
2.25	2 steel, B/1	☐
2.5, 2.75	C/2	☐
3.0, 3.25	D/3	☐
3.5	E/4	☐
3.75, 4.0	F/5	☐
4.0, 4.25	G/6	☐
4.5	7	☐
5	H/8	☐
5.5	I/9	☐
6.0	J/10	☐
6.5, 7.0	K/10.5	☐
8	L/11	☐
9	M, N/13	☐
10	N, P/15	☐
15	P, Q	☐
16	Q	☐
19	S	☐

To Learn More

Despite the promise on the cover, I do realize that I have not answered every question you'll ever have. It would take more than one small book to do that! However, there are many places you can go to learn more about crochet. Here are just a few resources for you to check out in more detail.

ONLINE

Type "crochet" in a search engine, and you'll get millions of hits! Because websites and podcasts appear and disappear with lightning speed, there's no way to list all of the good ones, but here's a list of sites to get you started.

Ravelry.com

Any discussion of online yarn-related fun has to start with Ravelry. Founded by Jess and Casey Forbes, this free social network is the go-to community for all things crochet, knitting, spinning, and weaving. It is a tool for organizing your personal yarn stash, a way to learn about yarns and patterns, and a community of passionate and knowledgeable fiber artists. With three million users and counting, the depth and breadth of communal knowledge is truly outstanding. New features and useful tools are constantly being added. As of the time of this writing, useful features on Ravelry include:

▶ A community-edited searchable yarn database that allows you to research both popular yarns and obscure, outdated yarns, and see what crocheters have made with them

▶ A community-edited searchable pattern database that includes hundreds of thousands of patterns in over two hundred categories

▶ Project pages where members post pictures and details of their finished projects, allowing you to see the same project completed in different yarns, as well as be alerted to possible problems with the pattern or challenges in stitching it

▶ The ability to create your personal searchable inventory of yarn, patterns, books, and projects

▶ Thousands of groups that you can join to chat with others who share your particular fiber-related interests (a few of the biggest for crocheters: Crochet on Ravelry, Crochet Liberation Front Headquarters)

www.crochet.org

The official website of Crochet Guild of America (CGOA) with a "how to crochet" section for both left- and right-handers

www.Crochetville.com

A welcoming, bulletin-board-based community

www.craftyarncouncil.com

Loads of resources from the Craft Yarn Council, including how-to illustrations and appealing projects

www.yarnstandards.com

Another Craft Yarn Council website; provides the Standards & Guidelines for Crochet and Knitting described in this book (page 377).

www.marlybird.com

Yarn Thing Podcast with Marly Bird (Note: There are many yarn-related podcasts. Share your favorites with me through social media.)

crochet.about.com

You could spend all day clicking the links from this site. You'll find free patterns, product reviews, yarn sources, beginner to advanced techniques, stitch dictionaries and charts. Even the advertising serves as a resource!

www.stitchguide.com

Explanations and illustrations of the crochet basics, plus more advanced techniques, all with a bonus: You can watch a video of each stitch as it is made. View clear close-up shots of hands, hook, and yarn, repeating the stitch over and over as many times as you need to understand and learn the technique.

LOCAL RESOURCES

At your local yarn shop, craft store, or library, you may find experienced crocheters willing to answer your questions. At stores, don't just limit yourself to the employees! Talk to other customers; you might be surprised at the level of expertise you find. Look for fiber arts guilds in your area, or start your own, meeting at a coffee shop or community center. Members can take turns learning new skills and teaching each other.

CLASSES

Classes on a huge range of topics are available online, some for just a nominal fee. Some offer the ability to interact with the teacher online. Your local library, recreation center, or community college might offer crochet classes, or you can take advantage of classes at yarn shops and craft stores. You might find someone willing to come to you for customized private instruction. There are also professional crochet teachers who travel to teach workshops in your community. Did you know that there are national crochet conventions, where people from around the country gather to share ideas and learn new techniques? There's really no excuse not to be learning more *all the time*.

www.craftsy.com

An ever-growing catalog of online classes in many types of crafts, as well as a pattern store. Sign up for a class, own it forever, and watch it in your own time. Ask questions and get responses from fellow students and from the instructor, including yours truly.

www.creativebug.com

Online classes in a multitude of disciplines, including crochet. Classes are offered on a subscription basis and à la carte.

www.knitandcrochetshow.org

> The convention of the Crochet Guild of America and The Knitting Guild of America, including classes and market.

www.knittinguniverse.com/stitches (Stitches Events)

> Multiple locations of the Stitches events throughout the year make it easier to find one that suits your schedule. Includes a yarn market and knitting and crochet classes.

DESIGNERS

Many designers are doing innovative and creative work; these same designers often teach online or in person. I couldn't possibly list all of them; if you have your favorites not listed here, please let me know! Find these designers on social media and through their websites:

Doris Chan
www.dorischancrochet.com

Edie Eckman
www.edieeckman.com

Kim Guzman
www.kimguzman.com

Jennifer Hansen
www.stitchdiva.com

Kristin Omdahl
www.styledbykristin.com

Stacey Trock
www.freshstitches.com

Myra Wood
www.myrawood.com

MAGAZINES

Check your newsstand for the crochet magazines
currently available.

Crochet! Magazine

Crochet World

Interweave Crochet

BOOKS

There are thousands of pattern books for crochet, and dozens
of how-to books in print. You can learn a lot from pattern
books; choose projects that use techniques you've never tried
before. Follow the instructions, and *voila!*, you've learned a
new technique. Stitch dictionaries are also fun for the budding designer. Here are the references that I use time and
again; each includes crochet symbol charts. And yes, I do
refer to my own books frequently!

Any Japanese stitch dictionary or pattern book you can get
your hands on

Eckman, Edie. *Around the Corner Crochet Borders* (Storey
Publishing, 2010)

——. *Beyond the Square Crochet Motifs* (Storey Publishing, 2008)

——. *Connect the Shapes Crochet Motifs* (Storey Publishing, 2012)

Hubert, Margaret. *The Complete Photo Guide to Crochet* (Creative Publishing International, 2014)

Kooler, Donna. *Donna Kooler's Encyclopedia of Crochet* (Leisure Arts, 2011)

Mountford, Deborah. *The Harmony Guide to Crocheting: Techniques & Stitches* (Three Rivers Press, 1993; out of print, but if you can find a used one, it's worth getting!)

Metric Conversion Chart

WHEN THE MEASUREMENT GIVEN IS	TO CONVERT IT TO	MULTIPLY IT BY
inches	centimeters	2.54
feet	meters	0.305
mils	millimeters	0.254

Index

Index

Page numbers in *italic* indicate illustrations.
Page numbers in **bold** indicate tables.